W9-DEJ-856

Divorcing with Children

DIVORCING WITH CHILDREN

Expert Answers to Tough Questions from Parents and Children

Jessica G. Lippman and
Paddy Greenwall Lewis

Westport, Connecticut
London

Library of Congress Cataloging-in-Publication Data

Lippman, Jessica G., 1941–
Divorcing with children : expert answers to tough questions from parents and children / Jessica G. Lippman and Paddy Greenwall Lewis.
p. cm.
Includes bibliographical references and index.
ISBN-13: 978–0–275–99311–5 (alk. paper)
1. Children of divorced parents. 2. Divorced parents. 3. Divorce—Psychological aspects. I. Lewis, Paddy Greenwall, 1945– II. Title.
HQ777.5.L54 2008
306.89—dc22 2007048777

British Library Cataloguing in Publication Data is available.

Library of Congress Catalog Card Number: 2007048777
ISBN-13: 978–0–275–99311–5

First published in 2008

Praeger Publishers, 88 Post Road West, Westport, CT 06881
An imprint of Greenwood Publishing Group, Inc.
www.praeger.com

Printed in the United States of America

The paper used in this book complies with the Permanent Paper Standard issued by the National Information Standards Organization (Z39.48–1984).

10 9 8 7 6 5 4 3 2 1

To Peter Lewis and Amelia Barrett, who provided us with inspiration.

Contents

Preface

As therapists, we have spent our professional lives listening to words that our patients have spoken—words of sorrow, lamentation, regret, despair, and hope. It is our hope that this book will help those going through divorce or contemplating a separation by listening to and learning from the words of others.

Between the two of us, in our more than fifty years of private practice, we have treated many adults and children whose parents have been through a divorce or are in the throes of a divorce. The stories we have heard from these people—wives, husbands, mothers, fathers, and children—demonstrate the loss, pain, and confusion that divorce causes. Many times, the people who sought help during this puzzling period have exchanged letters with us. The letters tell their stories during this time of distress: the destruction of a relationship, the feelings of betrayal, confusion, bewilderment, and fears of abandonment.

This book is a compilation of letters between people going through a divorce and their therapists. Brief introductions present problems that are common in divorce. The problems are illustrated with letters from patients. The therapist's response immediately follows and offers perspective, advice, and insight. The letters allow readers to understand how separation and divorce affect many lives: parents, children, friends, and family members.

The knowledge and insight we acquired from our patients is distressing, grim, and thought provoking. The individuals going through separation and divorce articulated and validated all that we had heard from other patients and from our academic studies in psychology. The letters painstakingly uncovered how their hurt and confusion have been misunderstood and distorted, and how it sometimes turned their lives and self-image inside out.

Statistics on the effects of divorce are both frightening and stunning. Two million couples marry each year. One million couples file for divorce every year, and over 70 percent of second marriages end in divorce. In the United States, 2.2 million people under the age of 35 get divorced. Our hope is that, by addressing this subject, we will help individuals to protect themselves from some damaging and alarming consequences that may occur during the disintegration of a marriage.

"Help me to find the words to tell the children" was the plaintive plea that spurred the idea for this book. "I feel like such a failure as a person and a mother—I feel like we're both floundering. Can you help me?" Some of the questions came in the form of e-mails or letters sent to us. And so the old-fashioned art of letter writing began in an effort to help with the dilemma of divorce. This book is a collection of correspondence between patients and their therapists. Practical and pragmatic advice is offered in response to the letters rather than theoretical answers. We share these rich letters from engaging personalities in the hope that reading individuals' actual stories will help others in similar situations.

The impact of separation and divorce on children can be very difficult. Children whose parents divorce (even in a so-called good divorce) grow up with their lives being ordered in a completely different manner than their friends who grow up with married parents. By addressing these difficult situations, this book will be helpful to parents who are coping with their children's problems.

The book is divided into sections. We first discuss the difficulties encountered in the crumbling of a marriage, beginning with the reasons people seek a divorce. The book next addresses the problem of how to explain the parents' divorce to a child. Other chapters discuss moving out, custody, parental alienation, the effect on families, and new relationships. The end of each chapter contains a number of golden rules. These also appear at the end of the book. The appendix includes a primer on the financial issues involved in divorce.

Every person who is going through a divorce, whether left or leaving, has to cope with the hurt and disappointment that accompany a failed marriage and the collapse of hope. Coming to terms with the grief means letting go. In divorce, this means letting go of all the shared identities over the time spent together. We hope that these stories of people going through divorce will help others facing similar struggles.

This book began many years ago and was interrupted by the events of September 11, 2001. At that time, we felt we wanted to help children who were coping with the death of a parent and addressed this in our book, *Helping Children Cope with the Death of a Parent: A Guide for the First Year*.

Acknowledgments

We are hopeful that this book conveys our commitment to the problems encountered by divorcing families as well as our dedication to helping with vital issues of divorce. This book is the product of the efforts and faithfulness of countless current and past patients and individuals who have shared their stories in order to help others. We could not have written this book without their honesty and their willingness to expose their pain.

We are both fortunate to have loyal friends and family who have provided inspiration and encouragement. We particularly want to thank Professor Matthew Lippman, who was a constant source of support and generous assistance. We are grateful to our parents, Solomon G. and Belle Lippman, and Jack and Sylvia Greenwall, who allowed us to grow up in intact families.

One

Reasons for Divorce

If I were married to you, I'd put poison in your coffee.

—Viscountess Astor

If you were my wife, I'd drink it.

—Churchill

At times divorce is inevitable. When there is violence, domestic abuse, alcoholism, or some other untenable factor present in the relationship, divorce sometimes seems to be the only solution. The *Diagnostic and Statistical Manual* of the American Psychiatric Association cites death and divorce as the two most stressful of the major psychosocial problems in life. It is not surprising, then, that deciding to divorce is a big decision, usually fraught with anguish on both sides. However, different people have different tolerances for dealing with problematic situations, and the decision to divorce may sometimes be made too lightly or appear so. There are many reasons why people choose to get divorced, some more serious than others: alcoholism, drug abuse, mental illness, physical abuse, sex, money, poor communication, and an inability to balance time spent with the family and at the job are among the most common. The top three problems that lead to divorce are sex, money, and time. Likewise, a variety of reasons may influence the decision to remain married: religious beliefs, family pressure, finances, or stoicism. A choice is then made to stay in a marriage despite the hardships.

Whatever the reasons for divorce, it is always disruptive to the couple and to the entire family. The children are always the collateral damage no matter what the reason for the divorce. Even when, for example, a child has witnessed abuse or severe alcoholism and can rationally understand the necessity for the divorce, there is still residual damage. The divorce is experienced as a death: the death of a family.

ABUSIVE RELATIONSHIPS

There are two forms of abuse in relationships—physical and mental—and both are equally damaging to the family. Abuse is destructive to the spousal relationship and traumatic for the children. The husband is usually (though not always) the physical abuser. Evidence suggests that abuse can occur in families over several generations; often abusers grew up in an abusive home. Children sometimes witness the abuse, or they can be the recipients of the abuse. The relationship between the parents is severely compromised when a child is a victim of abuse. This becomes a destructive cycle: one of the parents attempts to protect the child, the child tries to protect the parent, which further incites the abuser.

The letter and response that follow illustrate the ambivalence and guilt that are often felt by spouses who have experienced physical abuse.

Hi Dr. L.,

I wanted to update you. We have moved on to Kentucky and the children are all very happy. My sister has been wonderful helping us to buy a house and helping us acclimate to the community.

I know the kids miss their dad—I see it on their faces at soccer practice when there are other dads around, and they are even beginning to talk about missing him. But, as you know, he had been pretty physical with me for a long time, pushing me, hitting me, pulling my hair, and putting my head in a vise-like lock. The final straw, which you don't know about, came when he shoved me against the window and my hand smashed through the glass, cutting me from wrist to thumb. Eighteen stitches later I knew I had to get out. There was no way I was leaving the kids in his care. The kids had witnessed the screaming, the blood, the police, and the trip to the ER, and they had seen that scene once too often. I left that night for Kentucky.

Now that a few weeks have passed, and I see how much the kids miss him, I am beginning to doubt my decision about leaving. Did I overreact? Do you think we can work this out—do you think we should go back to marital counseling? Really looking forward to your email.

Debbie

Dear Debbie,

You know you have a 12-year history of continual abuse, recriminations, and forgiveness. You also have a history of being in marital counseling with Dr. B. for a couple of years. Despite his promises, nothing has changed. You and I, in your individual therapy, have talked many times about the self-esteem issues and the repetition compulsion (repeating your father's physical abuse of you) that have kept you in the marriage. You feel this is what you deserve and so keep returning to reinforce this belief. You must find a therapist in Kentucky to help you work on this issue. No one deserves to be pummeled and battered. Your children certainly do not need to witness the horror of it.

I know this is a difficult time for you, but I also know you have the inner strength to deal with it. Keep me posted.

Regards,

This woman, like so many others in her position, and in spite of all that has happened, feels ambivalent and guilty about leaving her husband.

Emotional abuse is as hurtful as and sometimes more destructive than physical abuse. Emotional abuse involves the denigration and demeaning of the partner. It can have a lasting effect, as vicious words are played over and over in the mind. Emotional abuse can take the form of partners who are constantly hypercritical, making their spouses feel inadequate, devalued, insecure, self-doubting, and inept. Emotional abuse crushes confidence and self-esteem and undermines the ability to trust. It causes preoccupation, which affects concentration and often leads to depression or severe anxiety. These all contribute to problems at work and in social situations. Sleep disturbances can occur, and physical health can be compromised.

A need to psychologically control a partner is a form of emotional abuse that can be deadly particularly when it is manipulative, constant, and unrelenting. For example, a wife who continually makes her husband doubt his sense of reality, setting him up over and over again, claiming, "I told you that, don't you remember anything." The fact may be that she never told him anything because her intent was hostile, wishing him to doubt himself and distrust his own perceptions and beliefs. Another example is a partner who shows no affection to the spouse but instead lavishes affection on a pet. Or demeaning remarks are made, such as "You are so stupid, do you know nothing! What are you, a sixth grader? They have that word in their vocabulary." Or "You always laugh like a donkey; I can't stand it. And you smell like a donkey, too. No one wanted to stand next to you at the party." The emotional abuse is constant, purposeful, intentionally hurtful, and designed to cause pain. It is directed at recipients' self-esteem and feelings of self-worth, making them doubt everything about themselves.

The following letter and response illustrate why people stay in destructive, emotionally abusive relationships: out of passivity, fear of loneliness, and feelings that they are worthless and unlovable.

Hi Dr. L.,

I finally did it. I called a lawyer. I couldn't stand it any longer. It was not only her lies and distortions about what she had told me, and her constant berating my ability to fund the lifestyle she deserved. (Even Steve was able to buy his wife a new car this year.) But I guess over the last couple of months when she began attacking my sexual prowess—that was it. She said such hurtful things that for days at work I couldn't concentrate and just heard her words over and over in my mind. I even began thinking, "I can't leave her because no other woman would want me." The vitriol of her words rings over and over. "You are such a terrible lover, maybe I should have married someone with experience. You will never please any woman." I feel so embarrassed, I'm not sure I could have told you this face to face in our next session, and I didn't want to wait a few weeks until I could finally get it out. This way you'll know ahead of our session and will help me talk about it.

Tom

Tom,

This must have been terribly painful. Her words are destructive and hurtful and are intended to cause pain and make you more dependent on her and make her even more in control. This is sadistic, and no one should have to subject themselves to such emotional abuse. Need I remind you, she also does this to the children. Remember when Lisa was all dressed up for a party and Sally said, "Take off that makeup; you look like a clown, and that dress shows how fat you are."

I am glad you had the courage to tell me about this. We will talk more about this in our session next week.

ALCOHOLISM AND DRUG ADDICTION

Alcohol poisons the liver, and it also can poison a marriage. It can lead to spousal and child abuse, loss of income, loss of job, loss of respect, lack of trust, loss of sexual relationships, and damaging behavior in general.

There are different types of alcoholic behavior ranging from the quiet functioning alcoholic, to a passive drinker who drinks until he passes out, to the boisterous "life of the party" who turns belligerent, to the falling-down drunk who is physically and emotionally abusive, to the extreme alcoholic who binges and disappears for weeks. No matter the type of alcoholic, the marriage and family are always affected.

Children are aware of the alcoholism, and it affects their peer relationships, self-esteem, and academic functioning. It is the well-kept family secret that affects all family relationships. No one in the family can depend on the person with alcoholism, leaving everyone vulnerable. Emotional unavailability is common to alcoholic behavior.

The following letter and response demonstrate the problems created in a household in which one of the parents has alcoholism.

Hi Dr. L.,

Well they split up. Strangely, I miss her. But I can't say I miss the nightly spaghetti dinner my dad made or coming home from school and finding her sprawled out in bed, dead drunk and snoring.

Do you remember my telling you about the one time I brought home a friend and she heard our laughter and came out of her bedroom, weaving and stumbling and slurring her words? I never brought anyone home again. I was so humiliated.

I want you to know I am now living with some family friends because my dad cannot take care of all of us. My new phone number is ______. I am not sure I can come to my next appointment. I don't know who can bring me. Please, please, will you call me? I feel so mixed up inside. I hate her, I love her, I'm sorry for her, but I'm glad the younger ones will not have to go through what I experienced. And, Dr. L., please help me to not become like her.

Jane

Hi Jane,

I'm glad you are safe and out of the chaos. Alcoholism is so destructive to a family. Look at what it has done to yours. No stability, no constancy, little nurturance, and constant bedlam, chaos, and unhappiness.

I'll call your dad and try to arrange for you to get here. Together we will try to understand your mom's alcoholism and how you can cope with it.

Regards,

The problems in an alcoholic household as typified by this young woman's letter tend to be persistent and can be passed down from generation to generation. The family system created may continue for many years, making for dysfunctional households where the misbehavior and abuse are considered normal. Children who grow up in dysfunctional families tend to adopt one of four basic roles:

The Good Child. This child is the responsible one known as the family caretaker, who learns to ignore his or her own feelings and to care for others.

The Problem Child. The family scapegoat, who is blamed for most problems.

The Lost Child. The inconspicuous, quiet one whose needs are often ignored or hidden.

The Clown. The child who brings a sense of relief to the tense family situation. This child's charming personality entertains others and gives the impression that stress is not a problem, while in reality the child feels frightened and alone.[1]

The following story was recounted by the mother of a nine-year-old boy who was plaintively reflecting on his father's alcoholism. As his mother was tucking him into bed, he told her that that day when flying a kite in the park with her he had seen a father flying a kite with his two young sons. He watched the father and wished that he were one of the sons.

> "I wanted him to be my father, and I was imagining what it would be like." He continued, "There is something missing when I'm with Dad." She asked him what was missing. He replied that when he was with his father he misses her but also something else he could not put into words. "It is sort of like he's not totally there like the other dad was."

This letter illustrates a husband's feelings of futility living with an alcoholic wife and the difficulties of moving forward with a divorce.

> Dr. L.,
>
> I just had a conference call with my sons. Anne fell Friday and broke her left arm, her dominant arm. She has fallen three times in the last week. (Alcohol.)
>
> We would like to have a session with you next Friday, as my son Jay is able to be in town that day. Let me know if you can schedule us for two hours, as there is so much to talk about.
>
> We are all struggling with Anne's deteriorating condition and return to full-blown addiction characteristics.
>
> We talked this morning about doing an intervention or getting her evaluated to determine if there is any long-term program that it would be worth committing her to in an effort to get her sober.

Our divorce date has been continued twice in the past two weeks, once because of Anne's attorney's having another pressing matter and Monday because Anne broke her arm. The boys and I decided that I should go ahead with the divorce as soon as she is able, since waiting only prolongs whatever reaction Anne is going to have as a result of the divorce becoming final. We can discuss all this on Friday.

Steve

INFIDELITY

Infidelity often destroys the marriage relationship because it destroys the most vital part of the marriage's fabric: trust. The sense of betrayal felt is profound and devastating, and little can be said or done to negate the harm done. Infidelity does not simply occur in a vacuum. There are always reasons underlying infidelity—some simple and some complex. These underlying reasons range from boredom to vindictive vengefulness.

Two of the top causes of divorce—problems involving sex and money—may also contribute to infidelity. Many arguments between couples have to do with money: the lack of it, the spending habits of one partner, the different values of the partners (risk versus security), and the frustration over different financial aspirations and ambitions. The fights and disagreements propel partners toward someone who seems to share or at least be more in tune with their own financial point of view. "I spoke to Mary at work, she would never spend over $100 on a pair of shoes." And "Why does Janey have to go to that summer camp that is thousands of dollars above our budget?"

Financial gain is often linked to infidelity. Women are most susceptible to this. The young, overworked secretary or lawyer, with children and husband and home to care for after her day at work, may well be tempted by an older successful man who can offer the hope of a life of financial ease.

The following letter and response describe a common scenario. A man and woman meet in college, fall in love, and marry. They grow in different directions, the marriage becomes untenable, and the situation leads to one partner's infidelity.

Hi Dr. L.,

It's good to be out of town spending the week with my sister. Gives me a chance to mull things over a little. But before I forget, I wanted to make sure to tell you a little more about my affair—we sort of ran out of time in our last session, and I didn't want you to think I was a shallow, money-grubbing little bitch!

The fact is that when Don and I met in our freshman year of college we were not only very attracted to each other, but also thought we viewed the world in exactly the same way. Our political beliefs were the same, we enjoyed the same books and movies, we came from similar backgrounds, and we both detested the fake kids who seemed to care only about appearances and money. "The golf and club set," as we named them.

Our marriage was great for a few years, probably until we were both in our late twenties. Maybe I changed, maybe I grew up? But after working incredibly long hours as a surgical nurse, I found myself getting more and more irritated with Don, who went from job to job, sometimes even being fired for perpetual tardiness. When I tried to talk about it, he would get defensive and sarcastic. "We can't all be devoted Florence Nightingales," or "Get off my back, there's more to life than work." I started resenting his attitude as I got up at 5:30 in the morning to dress and get to work on time while watching him lying in bed sleeping soundly, knowing he had not set his alarm and would be late for work again. Our arguments became fights, particularly when friends started buying condos and started having babies. I knew this would not happen for us on my salary alone.

And then one day a new resident joined our surgical team. I liked him immediately: his humor, his intelligence, his modesty, his incredible dedication to his patients, and, even when sleepless and exhausted, his sense of responsibility to patients. And we had so much in common, so much to talk about. I'd known him for over a year when he first suggested a cup of coffee in the canteen. That "coffee" lasted three hours. The rest, as you know, is history.

When I return, perhaps we can talk about what I should consider: doing marital therapy? separation? or what? I can't go on living like this, yet I feel frozen about any change. I know you've heard this many times and hope and trust you'll be able to help me resolve this.

Fond regards,

Dee

Dee,

Affairs are symptoms of what is happening in a relationship. I think you are feeling torn and disloyal to the man you fell in love with and married. When you were in college and first met, you had a lot in common. Perhaps you are right—you grew up and he did not. People sometimes grow in different directions. What we want in our twenties is not necessarily what we want later in life. Clearly, your work ethic, sense of responsibility, motivation, and drive are different from Don's. Of course, you would be attracted to someone who shares the same life philosophy as you.

You have a lot of questions to answer. Do you still love him? Could you live with him and continue in this marriage if he does not change? Do you think he has the capacity to change? Could you tolerate a marriage in which you would always be the major breadwinner? Would you be able to tolerate a life in which you could not have the things your friends have? These are questions you need to think about and answer for yourself in a nonjudgmental way. Until you have thought more about the questions that must be considered, issues such as separation or marital therapy are premature.

As a famous philosopher, Freud, once wrote, in order to have a balanced life, one must have both love and work.

We will talk about all of this when we next meet.

See you Wednesday.

The following letter illustrates the challenge of trying to create a timetable for the resolution of feelings that arise from divorce due to infidelity.

Dear Dr. L.,

Thanks for answering my last email.

I just want to say that I feel totally overwhelmed. My house is overflowing with things that I've intended to get to but haven't. I just cannot put away the scraps of memories that surround me, because I am afraid of throwing away my past, or forgetting it. So I hold on to every smidgen of paper and all the cards and letters that we sent to each other over the years. I feel like I have so much to plow through. I know that you are to going say it is my emotions and the attachment I still feel that is stopping me.

I wonder, does Jake feel selfish or guilty for what he has done to the kids, replacing us and me? He always interpreted my frustration and impatience with him as abuse. He doesn't know a thing about real abuse. I really wanted a chance to work through our troubles. But instead he chose to slot someone else into my place, and now he is gone from our lives.

I can't take all of this; I wish I were not here surrounded by all this mess. I am so discouraged. Shouldn't I have gotten through these feelings by now? Thanks for listening (reading).

Jill

Good Morning Jill,

There is no set timetable for getting over feelings.

The following section contains a young man's account of finding out that his mother had been having an affair and grappling with her remarriage.

My mom announced, in a Christmas Eve phone call to me and my brother, that she was divorcing our father and moving several towns away to a new house that was to be all hers. We were both dismayed, confused, and hurt by her announcements. We had never expected our parents to part and had no idea of any trouble between them. We thought we were the "perfect family."

Several months after the divorce became final, Mom confided to my wife in a phone call that she had a boyfriend with whom she was serious. Apparently, my mother had been having an affair with this man for a couple of years. Katherine dished with her about the new boyfriend but told my mom that she needed to tell me because she would not keep a secret from me.

Almost a year later, Katherine and I had a baby and invited Mom to come for a week to visit. We planned the visit and a time and date of arrival. The day before she was to come, Mom called and changed the plans all around: new day of arrival, new time, train instead of plane, and everything became really confused. It turned out Mom's new boyfriend was to accompany Mom on the train to Chicago, and he planned to turn around immediately and take the train back to Kansas City. We offered to pick her up at the train, but Mom said Larry had never been to Chicago and they wanted to sightsee before he got back on the train, and she would get herself to our house. We were really baffled by the new plans, and on the day she was to visit we sat in the living room to wait for Mom. We waited and looked out the window to see when my mom might arrive. While we were waiting and watching we saw a car pull up and a man opened the trunk and handed my mom a suitcase. Mom came into the house and we asked, "Who is the fellow who handed you your suitcase from the car?" Mom said it was Larry (the guy my mom is engaged to and whom I'd never met). Larry had rented a car and was now planning to return to the train station without coming upstairs and meeting us or seeing the new baby. We were incredulous.

We insisted on Larry coming in so we could meet him and so he could have a bite to eat before going back to the train. We ordered a pizza, and I have to tell you it was the most uncomfortable hour and a half I have ever spent in my entire life. Katherine tried to fill every silence with words. I mean she did not stop talking. Larry sat like a wooden solider on the couch barely speaking, and my mom sat with her hands folded in her lap real prim and proper like she got caught doing something she shouldn't have and I was like a stunned zombie. I was prepared to accept my mom's new boyfriend and the new relationship, but I have to tell you, my mom is really making this difficult!

Infidelity may stem from any one of a number of underlying situations, including (but certainly not limited to) sexuality, stress, substance abuse, mental or physical illness, and different cultural norms and expectations.

A couple's sexual relationship is pivotal to the success of the marriage. Infidelity is inevitable for couples who are not sexually compatible. Even when couples do enjoy a sexual relationship, there are times when one of the partners' interest in sex may be diminished. This can occur with the birth of a baby, the demands and intrusions of children, illness, fatigue, job stress, and other family and life problems. At these times, the marriage is vulnerable, and infidelity becomes a possibility. Infidelity is almost guaranteed when the sexual orientations of the marriage partners are different. Sometimes one partner is aware at the time of the marriage of his or her homosexuality; sometimes the preference for a same-sex partner is discovered after the marriage. Either way, infidelity is quite likely to occur.

Personality disturbances may sometimes account for infidelity. For example, a person who has a narcissistic personality disorder has an extremely heightened need to be admired, flattered, and pursued; a person suffering from a bipolar disorder may act out sexually and financially at times, and rationality and clear thinking are then severely compromised. When one of the partners in a marriage is beset with severe physical or mental illness, healthy spouses may find themselves in need of someone who is available to them. Depleted, lonely, under stress and pressure, they may find themselves reaching out to someone who can offer them companionship, nurturance, and support—a shoulder to lean on. Alcoholism or drug abuse can contribute to negative feelings about a spouse, and a relationship with a kind, sober, empathic person can quickly bloom into an extramarital affair.

Other problems and stresses such as work, in-laws, and child-rearing difficulties (especially where there is a lack of communication) can cause problems in a marriage. Stress, feelings of neglect, or lack of support from a partner can open the door to comfort from someone outside of the marriage.

The complexion of U.S. society has changed over the last 50 years. Immigration has created a society comprised of many different cultures and nationalities. As a result, marriages have become far more multicultural and multiracial. The blending of different cultural values, norms, ways of life, and diverse religious beliefs within a marriage can make for difficulties. Infidelity may even be viewed in different ways by different cultures: some regard it in an almost blasé manner, while others are deeply offended by it. Although we may initially be fascinated with the different and the exotic, living day to day with someone who has different ways of viewing the world or who has different ideas of child-rearing, male/female roles, or the involvement of extended family can make for stress and discontent. If the discontent is serious enough, the search for someone who understands, someone perhaps from one's own culture, is not unlikely.

PHYSICAL ILLNESS

People have different capacities for dealing with unanticipated complicated life situations. Their reactions should not be judged. Some people can carry more burdens than others. Physical illness puts a tremendous strain on the spouse and the family. Alzheimer's disease, multiple sclerosis, cancer, accidents that paralyze, debilitating illnesses, and any illness that robs the individual of independence and normal function create tremendous stress for the healthy spouse. Suddenly, a spouse has to deal with an ill partner, sometimes a virtual stranger, not the person one married, nor what one had bargained for.

In these situations, the marriage is totally changed—socially, emotionally, financially, and sexually. The entire dynamic of the relationship has shifted. There is no longer an equal partner or shared responsibility. Everything depends on the healthy spouse. Not surprisingly, this creates a strain on the marriage.

This letter and response describe the feelings of guilt that occur when one partner decides to leave a marriage with an incapacitated spouse.

> I'm sitting in Lois's room feeling so despondent. We came to Mayo because I hoped they would be able to offer something more positive than what we had been told previously. The diagnosis and prognosis seems the same as the one we got from Willowbrook Hospital. No, she will never function as she did before. She may regain some speech, but her mental capacity is permanently impaired, she will never be the same.
>
> Of course, I feel so terribly guilty. Because it was I who encouraged her to join me in motorcycling. We hoped that having a shared interest would bring us back together again. And we did have fun. She really was quite good, but it was one of those freak accidents. No one could have ever anticipated what happened.
>
> Even though we had only been in marital therapy with you a few weeks, I think you know we were really struggling with many issues. But I think you haven't known me long enough to understand I just cannot cope with this sort of thing. I was never particularly selfless or nurturing. I know myself well enough to know I just cannot do this.
>
> Our families, our kids, and our friends will never understand or accept what I want to do. How do I explain my decision to the kids? It seems so

heartless and, I guess, selfish. But then I argue over and over in my mind, "How can I be trapped with someone who needs care 24 hours a day and can give back so little?" We have two youngsters at home, and I am unable to be mother, father, and nurse. Am I rationalizing? Am I making too hasty a decision? Am I a horrible person?

Can you call or send me a note. My e-mail address is_____.

Hi,

You are reeling from the fact that the second opinion is not positive. It is really a very difficult decision but one that only you can make. Do not make any precipitous decisions. You are probably still in shock from all that has happened. Let things settle.

I would strongly advise you to talk this over with a professional. You may be able to cope with the situation, you may not. But, it is essential that you get professional help and a chance to deal with all of your emotions, including guilt. You will need a professional who has experience with children, because this will be very difficult for them. They not only need help with losing their mother, but any decisions that will be made about the marriage. If you need names of qualified therapists, feel free to call or write.

Regards,

MENTAL ILLNESS

Mental illness is a spectrum that runs the gamut from anxiety to severe depression to psychosis. It includes obsessive-compulsive disorders, demanding, exploitative, self-absorbed behaviors, and other personality disorders. Such illnesses can be exhausting and emotionally draining for anyone who encounters the behavior. Any of these conditions can cause havoc in or destroy a marriage.

Mental illness may not be apparent at the time of the marriage but may emerge after several years, leaving the spouse feeling bewildered and desperate. The fun young partner who turns into a specious, agitated, delusional person is both frightening and confusing. Severe mental illness with a poor prognosis can erode a marriage. The healthy spouse often feels guilty about abandoning a sick partner. However, divorce is not always inevitable. Some people are able to handle burdens in ways that others cannot.

This letter and response depict how one child handles the burden of a mentally ill parent.

Dear Dr. L.,

Today I thought of running away from camp, but then I thought I would write you first.

You know my mom has been in the hospital for a long time. When I went to say good-bye to her, she really scared me. She didn't even look the same. Her hair was all slicked back. She had no makeup on, and she was wearing funny clothes. When she saw me she started screaming, "My little girl is dead—why are you tormenting me?" I kept saying, "Mommy, it's me." And she sort of stiffened and pulled back; it was so scary and horrible. It was worse even than when I would be lying in bed and hear her screaming and screaming at night.

What was even worse is that on the ride up to camp, my dad said, "It does not look like Mommy is ever going to get better, I think we will never be able to bring her home. I know this is hard for you to understand, but she is very, very sick and I cannot care for her. She needs a hospital and doctors to look after her." I kept saying, "But Dad, I can help you take care of her." "No, sweetie, no," he simply said.

Dr. L., I do not know what to do, I just want to run away, maybe to Nana. Maybe she will know what to do. Please tell me what to do.

Annie

Hi Annie,

It must have been very scary to see your mom like that when you went to say good-bye. You must remember she is very, very sick and does not know what she is saying. Your mom loves you and has been a very loving mother when she was not sick. She does not know what is real and not real any more, and that is why she did not know who you were and said the sort of things she said. There is nothing that you have said or done to cause her to be sick.

I know this is a very, very hard time for you, but you have Nana, your dad, and me to help you try and understand it and get through it. Running away is not going to make any of this better. You will be home from camp next week, and you and I will be able to talk and talk.

This must be very hard for your dad, too. I think he is trying to do what is best for your mom even though it is really hard to understand right now.

I will ask your dad to call the camp director and arrange for me to call you in the next couple of days.

Regards,

The following letter is from a husband grappling with leaving a mentally unstable wife.

Dear Dr. L.,

I do not know if you remember me. I saw you a couple of years ago when I was doing my internship in Chicago. Since that time, I did a residency in gynecology, and I am now an obstetrician in a small town about 100 miles from Chicago. As you can imagine, my hours are horrific. But that is not why I am writing to you. The problem is my marriage. As you remember (and warned me about), Freda is self-centered and demanding. It is always about her. The other night I came home after 36 hours without sleep, and she insisted she wanted to go to the movies that night. When I put my foot down, she began screaming and throwing things even though I said we could go the next night. This was the final straw. The tantrum happened in front of the children, with no concern that her behavior might upset or frighten them.

To quote you, "It is always about her." I guess I hoped it would change. I thought you were being too critical. Guess not. She is demanding, relentless, unaware of others' needs, and has no concern of the effect she has on others. I know the movie story might sound like a small event, something you do not consider getting divorced over. But this kind of behavior occurs daily. She wants her needs gratified immediately regardless of the other person, the situation, or even reality. It could be something as small as wanting a light bulb put in for her NOW, or wanting to go to the store for a part for her computer.

She sets up situations where whatever you do is wrong, no matter how right it is in reality. Let me give you an example: she insisted I go with her to look for a new computer. No computer in the store met her requirements—they were either too big, or too small, or she did not like the screen, or, if you can believe this, the color did not match the color of her fax machine! This happened on my one day off—four hours looking for computers and walking out empty-handed. She had no clue why I was upset. And when my beeper went off, she threw a snit because it wasn't in her plans. It meant my attention was not focused solely on her.

So, I would like to come in and see you. I am free every third Wednesday. Can you fit me into your schedule?

Regards,

Paul

Paul,

Yes, this is very self-centered behavior; we would call this type of behavior a narcissistic personality disorder. It is indeed very difficult to live with.

I can see you on _____. We will talk more when we meet.

Regards,

GROWING APART

Many times people marry in their early twenties and later grow in different directions. Common interests are no longer shared, and new attitudes and awareness develop. The very thing that initially attracted may become annoying and irritating. Often what attracts us to someone initially becomes the source of difficulty and frustration later on and becomes the reason to end the marriage. A woman may be attracted to a man who is responsible, careful, and conservative only to later on find him boring and stultifying. Or a man may initially be attracted to a woman who seems warm and nurturing only later to find her constantly hovering and smothering.

The writer, actor, and director Woody Allen, in his 1977 romantic comedy of modern contemporary love and urban relationships, has the hero Alvy Singer tell Annie Hall when they are about to split up that a relationship is like a shark: "It has to constantly move forward or it dies. And I think what we got on our hands is a dead shark."

CULTURAL AND RELIGIOUS DIFFERENCES

Cultural differences at first can be attractive and exciting but can become problematic with time. For example, a man might be attracted to a woman's large, loving family. However, when he is expected to share his home with them, it may be problematic and difficult if he was reared in a culture that values boundaries and privacy. Different philosophies, values, and living styles may become a source in the breakdown of a relationship.

When first we meet and fall for someone, nothing seems insurmountable—not even different devout religious beliefs. Early on, what seemed feasible may become a source for arguments and problems in the marriage. With the addition of children, such differences can become more poignant and exaggerated. A young woman raised in the Jewish faith sighed, "I can't have a Christmas tree in my house; I thought I could do it, but I just can't. I know the kids would love it, but I can't."

These differences, if not addressed directly, can lead to insurmountable difficulties. Ideally, they should be anticipated before entering the marriage.

SEXUAL DIFFICULTIES

Although both love and sex are vital in a good marriage, many people enter marriage with unrealistic expectations and myths about love and sex, and the stresses of everyday life can interfere with the sexual aspect of a marriage. With the arrival of children, the sexual relationship goes through an adjustment. As gratifying as children are, they impose demands of time and energy, leaving less time for intimacy and sex. Job stress or loss, financial difficulties, illness, family problems, and issues with children all take their toll on the sexual relationship. It is at these times that communication between partners is absolutely essential. Without communication, distortions of the reality of the situation can take place: feelings are hurt, there are misunderstandings, people feel closed out. Arguments over doing the laundry, picking up clothes, and taking out the garbage are substitutes for what is really bothering the couple. People often do not recognize what is stressing them and causing the arguments. The garbage is not the issue!

If the lack of awareness and miscommunication continue, the difficulty intensifies, and frustration and anger build and begin to erode the marriage. Sex becomes the battleground of the relationship. Frigidity, impotency, premature ejaculation, faded passion, and differences in sexual appetite are a tremendous stress on any marriage. When these difficulties are not addressed professionally, they become the pathway to divorce.

Sexual problems are unsolvable when one of the partners is homosexual. Sometimes homosexual persons will enter a marriage hoping they can change or be changed, or sometimes they are not yet aware of their sexual preferences, or they simply want the "white picket fence" American dream. Family and religious pressures may have contributed to their choosing to marry. Homosexuals who attempt heterosexual marriage tend to leave their spouse and children feeling betrayed, hurt, angry, and devastated.

Despite the anger, hurt, betrayal, and shock, many partners feel relief when they find out that their spouse is homosexual. They finally understand what really has been wrong. Many women are criticized by their gay husbands for being too sexually demanding and are comforted to learn that they are not responsible for the sexual difficulties in the marriage. The following letter and response describe one woman's experience.

Dear Dr. L.,

I am so glad you agreed we could continue my therapy by e-mail and phone. As you know, I am completely without a support system, being here taking care of mother. This bicoastal back and forth brings back terrible memories, the memories of Dan's weekly travels back and forth between California and our home. And then Dan became too sick to travel anymore.

On the plane, I was flooded with memories of that period when I was taking care of Dan. Do you remember he had been so sick for weeks, and how I had to force him to go and see the doctor and then that terrible day when I found out he was HIV positive, and the truth of his homosexuality finally came out? And the lies at first on how he became infected? I felt so distraught, so betrayed, as if our whole marriage had been a lie. I am not sure I will ever be able to forgive him, and yet we really cared about each other.

I think about the clues that I missed. He never allowed me to choose any of my clothing, he insisted on choosing all the household furnishings, etc. I guess I just thought of it as his being controlling. But you were always suspicious and even questioned his sexuality.

Although I still have bad, bad days, I am beginning to feel alive again, and the kids seem to be doing well. Hope to hear from you soon.

Jenny

Hi Jenny,

It is interesting that going to take care of your mother brings this whole period back to you. You are taking care of your mother like you took care of Dan. Of course, it is difficult to forgive him given the whole subterfuge of the marriage. Sometimes it is too painful to see the reality of a situation until we are ready to see it. Sometimes we retreat from what we know. You had two children and did not want them to grow up without a father in the house. You cannot blame yourself for not recognizing his homosexuality.

Of course you feel overwhelmed. You are in the middle of a divorce (and having to deal with the reason for the divorce), taking care of a sick mother, and raising two children. You are also dealing with this terrible betrayal. Trust is going to continue to be an area of difficulty. We will work on this.

Regards,

Here a man describes his experience of learning that his parents were going to be divorced and discovering that the reason for the divorce was his mother's homosexuality.

I was eighteen. The call came from my father three weeks after they dropped me off at college.

My dad bluntly went straight to the point, as was his way. "Your mother wants a divorce." I was in shock. I had always thought we were a great family, a typical family, with no problems. My father worked hard and long hours as a trial attorney. My mother stayed home, and, when we kids were in school, she played tennis, swam, and ran around with her friends. She had a best friend, Janet, and we and Janet's husband and kids were always together—going to the club, picnicking on the beach, camping, skiing, and even traveling to Europe together.

My parents never fought, they seemed to get on well, they laughed a lot, talked a lot, had a lot of friends. They even golfed together! Divorce seemed one of those things that happened to other families. Not to us.

I don't think I said much to my dad in that telephone call. I didn't ask questions, and he seemed eager to get off the phone. Maybe he was as shocked as I was. For the next few weeks I was sort of a zombie, just going through the motions of going to class and staying up late at night drinking beer and partying. I don't remember even thinking about it. The weird thing was my mother and I never talked about it—she never called, and I didn't call her.

It was only when I went home for Thanksgiving that I was forced to face it. And that's when I found out the reason for it all: my mother and Janet were moving in together after having had an affair for years and years. That was fine with me. I liked Janet. No, I didn't mind, it was fine. I was glad she was happy.

My wife says I've never dealt with the divorce or my mother's homosexuality. She thinks the problems in our marriage are related to it. She says I'm wooden and can't communicate. I think she's wrong. I don't think any of it affected me after the initial shock of it all.

PORNOGRAPHY

Interest in pornography may be viewed as a form of infidelity. It also can be an addiction. Both can create tremendous stress and strain on a marriage. When one spouse views pornography in secret, the spouse who discovers this is left feeling angry, confused, and betrayed. The discovery of pornographic obsession often leads to divorce.

GOLDEN RULES

1. Think over the decision to divorce very carefully. Romance, excitement, and passion do not necessarily last. There need to be very real reasons for a divorce. Many lives will be altered, and divorce affects children for the rest of their lives.

2. Before rushing for a divorce, it is wise to try couples therapy.
3. Reach out for help for the children. Often children of divorcing parents are angry or scared, and they need help with understanding their feelings. If they misbehave, they may need some help in expressing their feelings with words rather than through behaviors. An objective, trained third party may be the answer.
4. Be aware of your own needs. Many parents who are in the throes of a divorce are so involved with helping everyone else through the divorce that they forget about themselves. If necessary, seek help for yourself with a trained professional or reach out to friends and family.
5. Examine and be honest with yourself. Is the cause of your unhappiness your marriage, or is it something else?
6. Don't rush into the decision to divorce. Maintain flexibility and an open mind. What looks like a problem today may not be viewed as a serious problem in the future. Listen to your inner feelings. Consider what attracted you to the person in the first place, and explain to yourself what happened to this attraction.
7. Consider what your life will be like without your spouse. There are financial and social consequences.
8. Be practical. The divorce process is not as easy as you might think. There are often battles over child custody, property, pensions, temporary financial support, and taxation.
9. Do not glamorize the single existence. Are you prepared to live life as a single parent, assuming much more responsibility for caring for children on a daily basis?
10. Be honest about how you contribute to the difficulties you are experiencing.
11. Make up your own mind. Do not let others influence you and so determine the future of your marriage.
12. Divorce is forever. Remember, once you are divorced, it is difficult to undo.
13. Think before you act. Think about the impact of divorce on your immediate and extended family.

Two

How to Tell the Children

If I can stop one heart from breaking,
I shall not live in vain.

—Emily Dickinson

Telling the children of the decision to divorce is perhaps one of the most difficult aspects of getting divorced. Parents are usually very protective of their children; they do not want to see their children unhappy or in pain. Knowingly to inflict pain on one's child is one of the hardest things for a parent to do. Sometimes compounding the problem of telling the children is the fact that, prior to officially announcing the decision to divorce, there may have been discord and fighting in the home and the child may have asked, "You're not getting a divorce are you?" to which the parent may have answered no. Now the parents may feel that they have lied to and betrayed the child. Parents are often at a loss about which words to use and are uncertain of when to tell the child.

The age of the child dictates the words used to explain an impending divorce. Children who are under two years of age when the parents separate sometimes engage in intense searching behavior for the absent parent. Crying and a short-lived separation anxiety often accompany this searching. Transitional objects are soothing to the child at this age. Children need to understand that the parting parent has not been tossed away and that the parent has not abandoned them. This is the age when a child learns to trust. Very simple language should be used in telling very young children.

> You will see both Mommy and Daddy all of the time, but we will not all live together in the same house. Daddy has a new house. You will visit Daddy in his new house and he will visit you. Everyone will be fine. You will go to the park with Daddy like you always do, you will go to toddler's swimming with me like you always do.

Two of the chief concerns for children from 2 to about 10 years of age are "What will happen to us?" and "Who will take care of us?" Assure children that their needs will continue to be met. Children may also have extreme fears of something bad happening to either parent (dying, being in a car crash, disaster striking).

Many times two- to four-year-olds question where the absent parent is; not always satisfied with the answers that are given, the child may ask the same question over and over again. Reassurance needs to be constant. Hyperactivity and vigilance are frequently observed in youngsters of this age, as are complex fantasies about the cause of the divorce and ideas about what will happen in the future. Two- to four-year-olds are able to grieve over their loss if proper support is provided to them. Very young children have no concept of time and distance. It is important to be concrete when telling the child when they will next see the parting parent. For example, circle a date on a calendar to show them when they will next see the parent.

Children who are four to five years old tend to have a complicated set of fantasies about why it happened and have wishes for a parental reunification. Young children feel omnipotent and think they have the ability to control the world. They feel they can make anything happen, including things such as separations and reunifications.

Children of this age may feel disloyal and guilty when they long for the absent parent or feel remorseful in accepting pleasure from a parent substitute. Children are concerned about the absent parent and want to care for that person, but they are also fearful of losing their custodial parent so are fearful of expressing how they feel about the now-absent parent. The custodial parent needs to encourage the child to express his or her feelings and be supportive of the child's sadness at the loss.

It is important for parents to help children resolve the feeling of perceived rejection that they might feel from the parent who left. Youngsters need to understand the why of a divorce in a concrete and uncomplicated age-appropriate manner so they can attempt to understand the current situation more fully.

> I know that you have heard Mommy and Daddy fighting a lot. If we do not live together, we will not always be arguing and fighting with one another. Mommy and Daddy love you and want to be with you. Because Mommy

and Daddy will not be living together and will be divorced, we cannot both be with you all of the time.

It is of utmost importance that children be assured that they will not be sent away like the absent parent, and that they are not responsible for the separation or divorce. The child needs to understand that the adults are unhappy with each other; they are not unhappy or angry with the child. Children also need to be reassured that if they argue or are angry with one of the parents, they will not be sent away like the absent parent.

Youngsters of 6 to 10 years of age understand that they are prized and loved by both of their parents. They can understand that their mother and father may not be able to stay with one another, but they may still wish for a reunification. Other children of this age, despite the guilt they feel, attempt to manage their loyalties to both parents. It is not uncommon, however, for some children to have a very intense grief reaction.

Adolescence is a time when children require firm limits and structure. Divorce compromises the security of stability and structure. In an attempt to find the stability and structure that are missing at home, particularly when the parents are temporarily unavailable because of their own difficulties, children of this age may turn to their peers more than usual.

It is fairly common for adolescents to have a volatile relationship with their parents, and, when parents separate and divorce, teenage angst and testing of limits may be exacerbated in a volatile manner. Adolescents who are prone to depression may see their parents' difficulties as an indication that adult men and woman cannot make each other happy, and this then becomes an indication that they have nothing to look forward to or to count on in their future. Some adolescents, unable to deal with the home difficulties, find any excuse to be away from home. Unlike younger children, teenagers sometimes experience difficulty in talking about future eventualities.

It is important for parents to convey to their children that, although divorce is difficult and disruptive, it is better than the parents continuing to live together in discord and making the whole family unhappy. Divorce will permit each of the parents to seek a better life, and this requires that they live separately.

Children of all ages are aware that Mommy and Daddy fought a lot, and they nurture fantasies of their parents being back together, but this time not fighting. When questioned, many children sadly add that they realize that their parents are unable to stop fighting, and so the fantasy is unlikely to become reality.

Meg, age six and a half years, reports her memory of when her parents separated, when she was 15 months old. This account was verified by her mother, who was shocked that Meg had any memory of the event.

> I remember them yelling and after that they took off their wedding rings and then they got divorced. They yelled really high, and all of a sudden I just felt my mommy take me into her room. Divorce means they will not be with each other again. I felt sad.

Sometimes children have clues that the marriage is in trouble; sometimes they do not. Some marriages are volatile, some are icy and silent, and some are sealed tightly, giving no hint of discord. And yet because the thought of losing a parent to a divorce is so devastating, children defend against such clues or messages and are traumatized when they hear the news. Some children even claim, defensively, that they felt relieved when they were told, because the household had previously been so chaotic and now it would be peaceful. It is only later, sometimes years and years later, that the impact and loss are truly felt.

Here a woman remembers her parents' divorce. She was 11 years old when it happened.

> At the time my parents told me they were separating, I was embarrassed that they were not going to be together, and I would not tell anybody. It was the public persona versus the private persona. When my parents told me they were going to be divorced, I was relieved. I was relieved that there would not be any more fighting, but the private relief was different from the public face. The first person I told that my parents were not together, I remember that my face became flushed, and I felt completely exposed. I can remember exactly where I was, every detail. I can even remember the smells around me.
>
> I think my father participated in my life more once they separated. I certainly never remember him attending any event in my life, ever. My mother took me everywhere and waited for me, not him. He was never really part of my life before the divorce.

When telling children about a separation or divorce, it is ideal if both parents discuss and agree on how and when to tell the children. No matter what the discord, the explanation should be simple and uncomplicated, and free of accusation, blame, and emotion. Calmness from the parents helps the child.

The parents also should agree beforehand on the reasons they will give the children for the divorce, what will happen and when, where everyone will live, and talk about any changes that might take place in the child's life (for instance housing, school, schedules). Ideally, both parents should gather all the children and tell them all at the same time. It is important for parents to tell the children that there is finality to the decision to divorce and so avoid giving children false hopes that the parents will reunite. In many cases, a script can be helpful. During this conversation, it is important to ask children to voice their concerns and fears.

The following letter describes a mother's concerns and questions about how to tell her children, and the response provides some guidance.

Dear Dr. L.,

It seems it won't be long now before we have to tell the children. I dread the thought. They seem so happy in their little world and now the bubble is about to burst. I feel so torn, so guilty, so scared. Last night I watched them together—they looked so content as he read them a story. "Daddy, Daddy show me that picture again, the one with the dragon. Dad, did he really save them all?" John Sr. was patient and sweet and loving. I looked at him and thought, "Oh my God, what am I doing?" But, as you know, it's an impossible situation with his drinking.

My question now is, when do I tell the children? Is there a good time, a better preferred time? And how do I tell them? What are the words? Late at night I play possible words over and over in my head. Nothing seems right! Give me the words! Please!

As you know. John is 10, and going into fourth grade, Katie is 6 and going into first grade. Given the difference in age, do I tell them together, separately? What? And should John Sr. tell them with me? Should we do it together? I'm not sure he'll agree to this. Needless to say, I dread the thought.

Well, thank goodness I have an expert to ask! I look forward to your answers—I know they'll be helpful.

Regards,
Callie

Dear Callie,

Yes, there is a good and preferred way to tell the children. A rule of thumb to follow is: never at bedtime, never before school, and only when there is plenty of time for reflection and plenty of time for discussion (conversation). Timing is crucial. As in all traumatic situations, time is needed to digest upsetting information.

You ask how to tell the children. Here is a sample script you could use. "Dad and I have something to tell you, something that will be difficult and upsetting to you. You know that there has been a lot of arguing between us that has been upsetting for everyone. After a lot of talking and thinking, Dad and I have decided that it would be best for everyone if Dad and

I lived in separate houses. We are going to be divorced; that means we will no longer be married to each other. You must remember we both love you a lot and we always will, and we will always be your parents, and you will see both of us all the time."

Clearly, there will be more questions. Answer them simply and as honestly as you can. I think you should tell the children together. Having both parents will provide some comfort to the children. If you tell them separately, you run the risk of them feeling they have to keep a secret from the other parent; or they may, in shock, run to the other parent and blurt out their understanding of what is about to happen, which would add more chaos to the situation. But would John be willing to sit down and calmly plan this with you? Or would he become volatile and defensive and say awful things about you? You know him better than I do, so given the above, you will have to make the final decision as to what is best. It would be ideal to have him there. Should he have a negative reaction, however, you'll have to pick up the pieces. If you decide to do it alone, you cannot be mean-spirited or emotional. Be calm and clear and use simple language. He may have a reaction, so you need to be prepared to deal with it as calmly as you can.

Regards,

In the following letter, Callie reports on how she and her husband carried out the task of telling their children about their divorce and wonders how to take the next steps.

Dear Dr. L.,

Thank heavens the ordeal of telling the children is over. It was painful in every way. The children looked so sad, and John and I were tense and unhappy. It wasn't supposed to end this way. John Jr. looked straight ahead, said very little, and when we asked if he had questions, he simply shouted "NO, and I hate you" and ran from the room. Katie, halfway through "the talk" started to cry and curled up in my lap and then, after a few minutes, went over to John and curled up in his lap and said, "I love you, Daddy. Please don't go." It was heartbreaking to say the least.

We struggled through the rest of the day. And as you suggested, I later asked both kids if they had any questions, if they wanted to talk more. Both seemed not to want to talk further today—were they digesting the news or simply hoping and trying to make it go away?

When I tucked them up in bed, both were a little tearful but with assurance that we both loved them, that they were not at fault, and that they would continue to see both of us a great deal. They seemed to calm down and go to sleep, though Katie did come and crawl in beside me in the wee hours of the morning.

And so now, we face the next big step. Moving out. How do we handle this? I know it's going to be so hard, if not traumatic, for the kids. Probably hard for me too! How do we do this in the best possible way? I'm eager to hear your thoughts.

Thanks so much for all the advice to date.

Fond regards,
Callie

Dear Callie,

So pleased it went as well as it did. Yes, we definitely will have to talk at length about the moving-out process. Will write more later.

Regards,

Sometimes, however, situations are not ideal. One of the parents may have already abandoned the family without warning. It is then up to the remaining parent to attempt to explain the desertion in unemotional, simple terms. Sometimes the relationship between the parents is so volatile that it may be impossible for them to sit down calmly together, let alone plan a strategy. In these volatile situations, parents should put their children's needs first and try to proceed in a civilized manner. When this is absolutely impossible, one parent will no doubt tell the children precipitously, and the other parent will have to pick up the pieces. A neutral third person's presence, such as a therapist, may be helpful.

At times parents who have agreed to a plan suddenly cannot hold their emotions in check and will begin hurdling accusations or blame at the other parent or saying that the divorce is something they don't want. Emotions may get out of hand, there may be weeping or yelling or fleeing the room and slamming doors, or threats. The calmer parent then has to take over and try to explain to the children; they not only have to tell the children about the divorce but have to try to comfort them as well.

The following section is a father's description of telling his children of his and his wife's impending divorce.

I dreaded telling the children. Josh was 10 and Sarah was 7. They were good kids, they didn't deserve this. But after meeting Sandy at a biotech conference a couple of years before, and seeing her on the sly every chance I got, I knew I had to get out of my marriage. I couldn't stay in a sexless marriage. I knew I was being selfish, but I knew I had to get out.

Tracy and I had talked to a family therapist about the best way to tell the children. So one Saturday morning, Tracy and I called the children into the family room and told them we needed to talk to them. We explained that we both loved them very much and always would, but that we no longer loved each other in the way we once did and that we were going to get a divorce. Although Tracy and I had sort of rehearsed what we would say, Tracy suddenly burst out—and this was obviously not a part of our script—with "Tell them the truth Rick, you've got a girlfriend." The kids handled it very well. They didn't say much, they didn't ask questions, and after a while I think it was Josh who said, "I need to get ready for soccer" and got up and left. Sarah followed him out of the room.

Here are the stories of a woman and a young girl recounting their similar experiences of being told about their parents' plans to divorce.

I knew something was very wrong even though I was only seven at the time. It must have been the "serious voice" that alerted me to the danger ahead. I don't remember much about what my Dad said to us, maybe I just blocked it out because it was so painful, but I honestly don't remember much of the beginning of the family meeting. The part I do remember is my mom yelling at him about his girlfriend, my mom bursting into tears and running out of the room.

I ran after her begging, "Mommy, Mommy, please don't cry, please don't cry." She clutched me to her and sobbed. That's all I remember. I don't really remember him telling us they were getting divorced or much else, I just remember my mom being distraught. The next few months are a blur.

Here, the seven-year-old girl recounts how she was told of her parents' divorce. Molly's mother was separated from her father. They had been married for seven years. They had not told their daughter that they had finally made the decision to divorce.

I had been spending the afternoon with my father and was scheduled to return to my mother's house in the early evening. We walked in much earlier than anticipated. There we found my mother and her boyfriend together. Enraged, my father said, "Meet your new father, Molly." I became hysterical and fled to her room. And that's the way I was told that they were going to be divorced.

The following letter and response address the issue of children's coping with the aftermath of learning of their parents' intent to divorce.

Hi Dr. L.,

How are you? Thanks for agreeing to help me with Janie and Sean. The situation is this: we told the kids we were splitting up about a month ago. Sean was okay, emotionally he seemed/seems fine, though he wouldn't articulate things as well or as often as Janie. At the time we told them, Janie was very upset, she cried a bit, saying she didn't want us to split up, but became excited at the thought of Daddy's new house and all the great things he said he was going to get her/do for her. Sean just wanted to watch TV!

In school, since she started, four years ago, Janie would have been one of the more emotionally immature children, crying at loud noises in the assembly hall, or if there was a new speaker for an assembly she would have become distressed easily. In the classroom, she would cry if she didn't get first in things—part of me believes, perhaps quite unfairly, that Janie expects to earn first in everything, or be praised for everything, just because she's Janie. She might not be very good at art, but would expect to get first prize, for example. This crying, etc. had, for the most part, stopped. She was coping with school well, as you know, and she's excellent at English and reading and really likes school.

In the two weeks preceding our telling the children, Janie's crying began again, over little things—like, for example, in class they would have a times-table contest and despite doing really well, beating her own scores and the scores of others, this wasn't good enough—I think she desperately craves attention, praise. Her teacher pointed this out to me, and that's when we decided to tell the kids. Janie listens to everything and most probably picked up on some of Rick's and my talks and arguments.

Since we told them, Janie and I have read the book *Dinosaurs Divorce* and have a policy of "any questions, any time," but she's had a couple of days when she's been dreadful at school, fighting, shouting, and crying; her teacher says she's very angry. Janie's temper is frightening to me and to others. Because of the depth of her feeling, it's like when she's angry she wants to rip everything to shreds, and, having had self-destructive tendencies like that myself, I worry that she'll choose that route. Last week she threw a huge tantrum in Burger King; she shouted and screamed and was so emotionally in shreds that it frightens me. I am very strict, and I put a huge emphasis on manners. So on the one hand, I know she has to express herself, but on the other hand, I want her to show respect and manners.

Often Janie's tantrums are random. She loses her temper when I'm telling her off for something, or even if I'm just asking her for something. If she doesn't like it, her world disintegrates and she loses it. I don't know how to deal with that. I don't shout—I used to, but now I don't raise my voice. I speak firmly but still she loses it. I don't know how to stop her having a tantrum, I don't know what punishment is applicable. I think that such displays of temper need some sort of punishment; usually she is sent to her room. She does get warnings. I don't punish or reprimand her on the first go, but today she is in her room. I don't know that it is a deterrent—if that's what's needed—I feel like such a failure as a mother, I feel like we're both floundering. Can you help me? I really appreciate you taking time to write me and help with Janie.

My questions would be: how do I react in a way that doesn't escalate my or her anger? How do I act when she's raging against anything? Do I take away her books or what?

What are the other questions that I should ask her that will allow me to get insight into her head (I don't know that she has the skill or the self-belief to be able to articulate her feelings)? I've told her that I won't be angry at anything she says, and I think she believes that. She did tell me she was mad at Rick and me for separating.

I think that's me all written out. I'd be very grateful for any advice you can give me regarding this.

Thanks,
Love,
Kitty

Kitty,

She is angry and confused and does not know how or what to do with the emotional overload she is feeling. She erupts randomly probably because thoughts often occur randomly as they cross her mind. Also she probably is very angry at you because she feels you are the source of her unhappiness. She probably blames you for the separation from her dad. The parent that the child is living with most of the time is usually the one that receives the brunt of all the anger. The parent who leaves is the one the child feels they have to "court" for fear of losing that parent completely. So the parent who leaves often does not see the child who is angry and upset but gets the compliant child.

Continue to tell her that you know she is feeling angry and unhappy and confused. Explain that angry words directed at you do not solve any difficulties, only make things more difficult. She is allowed to tell you that she is angry at you, but acting out her feelings will only get her a time out in her room. I would not remove the books in her room. The books may comfort her and help her to calm down a bit. I realize you feel the books are a reward for negative behavior, but at this time they are her only available comfort. If she likes to draw, suggest that she might try drawing a picture that will tell how she is feeling.

She might like writing a story about a girl who feels misunderstood, sad, and angry. Give her an outlet for her feelings. Is she involved in any physical activity that allows an outlet for her rage? This may help dissipate the anger. Also remember that often a young raging child is comforted and calmed down by being held by the parent for a while. When calm, they may then be able to talk more lucidly about their anger. At the time of the outbursts, they may too overwhelmed by emotion to think or talk coherently.

I think that she may be attempting to elicit punishment because she may feel that she deserves to be punished because she is the cause of the breakup. Remember, I told you children feel they are omnipotent, that they are the cause of all good and all bad things that happen. Did she tell Rick something about you and Ned that she feels may have caused things to go awry? At any rate, these are my thoughts. Tell Janie again and again she did not cause the problems between you and Rick.

Do not feel there is something wrong with your mothering. You are saying the absolutely correct words. Tell both of the children that you love them. Assure them of your love. Tell them, "All of us are going through a difficult adjustment. We will all make it through because we all love and care about each other." Most important, tell them that they can tell you what they are feeling and thinking, and encourage them to talk. Tell them you may not be able to make the feelings go away, but at least you can talk about what is bothering them. Talking makes it better. Maybe you can come up with solutions, maybe not. Let them know that together you will try to understand why all of you are feeling and thinking as you do.

Regards,

The following letter—from Juliet, who was 18 years old and away at college—is another example of the importance of telling the children about a divorce in the correct (or, in this case, incorrect) way.

Dear Dr. L.,

Hold onto your seat . . .

The other night I was awake for hours after my dad called to tell me that my mom had served him with divorce papers at his office. He was absolutely distraught, and I was truly worried that he might harm himself. He sounded like he was unable to function.

Mom had him served and then disappeared. No one knows where she is or how to get hold of her. Her sisters and brothers will not tell us where she is. Maybe they don't know either. No one has heard from her for a week.

I guess my mom asking for a divorce should not have been any surprise to me. I know that the marriage has not been happy for a long time. My mom is always trying to take me aside and tell me all the "bad" things my dad is doing to her. In front of him she is always praising his goodness, but behind his back she is busy destroying him. Behind her back, my dad always tells us how wonderful she is. Opposites?

Her behavior at Thanksgiving was strange, but she has acted like this before. Over my Thanksgiving break from college, we were all at my dad's family for the holiday, and she started her usual complaints that my dad was not "protecting" her or standing up for her in front of his family. We all have heard this complaint so many times that all of us thought "she's just doing it again," and we ignored the grumbling. The really weird part was that she was in a really agitated state and was constantly scribbling notes on little scraps of paper. At the airport while waiting for our flight back home, the two of them got into a gigantic argument, and the three of us kids wanted the floor to just swallow us up. None of us knew what was making her really angry; we just knew she has done this kind of thing before.

Anyway, my father was absolutely crushed, and after I got off the phone I found myself crying and devastated as well, even though for years I knew the marriage wasn't good.

I guess because my parents' marriage was such a difficult one and the divorce came as such a shock, I find that now I fear being dependent on anyone, and I don't trust others. I want to be the person who is lusted after, rather than the one being cheated on.

Juliet

Anastasia, Alexandra, and Nicholas were 11, 10, and 8, respectively, when their father told them that he and their mother were going to be divorced. Because the parents had separated and reunited on several occasions, the memory of this announcement is blurred. However, Alexandra, now an adult, remembers it this way:

> We were in the kitchen of my father's apartment when he told us that there was something he needed to speak to us about. He then told us of the impending divorce. I was in tears, my older sister began giggling out of anxiety (she had the closer relationship with our father and does not remember giggling despite the fact that my father has verified this), and my younger brother, Nicholas, plaintively asked, "Who will be our daddy now?" Today as an adult he remains a lost soul.

The children, in their own way, demonstrated their despair and desperation. No longer was the dream or wish of reunification alive; the divorce as presented was final and definitive.

The following letter and response delve more deeply into the experience of Kitty and Rick and their children. Kitty was earlier concerned more about her daughter, but here she describes her son's difficulties in coping with the divorce.

> Hi Dr. L.,
>
> Thanks for your e-mail; I'm sorry it's taken me so long to return your letter—maybe a bit of denial creeping in?
>
> At the time Rick and I were having problems—seems like we've lived the last four years in that state of tension. I wasn't aware that Sean picked up anything was wrong—I know that children will always pick tension up, but he seemed oblivious, and Rick and I didn't do (much) loud talking, certainly not in front of the children. School was maybe difficult; he tends to have an unsettled period at the beginning of each school year, getting used to a new teacher, new school friends, new rules, and, of course, the work. Sean is very smart, but he doesn't like to work too hard and will do the very minimum. If he likes a subject, he'll work harder, but writing and concentrating are ongoing struggles. I don't know if there was anything going on at school. Sean has never mentioned anything.
>
> Recently (I've been writing and thinking about this for some time, I think it's at least a month since I began this letter), whenever Sean's been upset, if I've been cross with him, he gets very, very upset—the worst crying I've seen from him in a long time. He says he misses his daddy, loves his daddy. I ask (and I know I'm doing this wrong), "What's better about Daddy's house?" and he says, "Daddy has a big TV (42-inch plasma!)," and Daddy lets him sleep in his bed, and Daddy lets him play PlayStation (the reason for the

first episode of crying came when, for the second time in three weeks, he was playing PlayStation and he didn't get to the toilet in time and wet himself a tiny, tiny bit). But Sean could NOT tell me, you know? So I said, no PlayStation for a day, and how I was very sad that he, a big, nearly 10-year-old boy, wet himself when that's what boys of three or so did.

I know I handled it badly. Wetting himself because he was too involved to go to the toilet is unacceptable to me. Anyway, he understood that this was his punishment, but when he went to bed he started crying, and that's when it all came out. He also said that Daddy doesn't shout at him as much as I do. (Rick would let the kids get away with an awful lot more than I would.) So I understand that he wants the big TV in Daddy's house and all the good stuff that goes with it. When he's not upset, he's very settled here (as far as I can tell). He never says that he misses Rick. I asked him what could we do to change things and make him not sad. He said that "Daddy has a big TV and a special computer chair, and they get to watch TV when they eat." I've told him that I can't get a big TV or a special computer chair. I explained that I do get cross sometimes, but he knows the rules in my house, and that he's a very smart boy and knows LOADS of stuff. I would try to be less cross, especially when I've done my night shift and haven't slept, and explain that he should try to help mummy and perhaps think before he does things. This sounds very dictatorial. It's not. It's just that Rick doesn't discipline the kids the way I do, and I think he gets less stressed with them anyway.

I know I'm rambling on. It's all so complex with Sean. I thought that Janie would be the problem, but it's Sean. I know he misses Rick, but I know he doesn't cry for me or miss me when I'm not there. Not that I'd want him crying, but I feel like I'm subjecting him to an awful torment of being with me. I have a friend who says that Sean's manipulative—not that he means to be, but that he's smarter and more astute than I give him credit for. I don't know whether he's unconsciously doing it or as, my sister Josie says, that the crying for the good things at Daddy's is his only means of articulating what he feels. I don't know what to say to him, other than reassure him that I love him and think he's brilliant . . . and of course he misses Daddy. But I feel like I'm floundering, and I'm going to damage him emotionally. Help!

Kitty

Dear Kitty,

This is what I suspected was part of what provoked the initial behavior. Do not feel there is something wrong with your mothering. Sean is crying because he is unhappy, frustrated, and/or angry. This is what happens when people are despondent. Give him plenty of support. For instance, you might say, "I know this is difficult for you. I wonder if it is difficult for you because you do not always enjoy writing and paying attention to subjects that are not your favorites. But it is something you need to do. You are a very smart boy and you need to show the teacher and yourself that you can do things that are not always fun." Understandably, you were upset that he went to bed crying.

You asked Sean what you could do so he would not be sad. Excellent. You were listening to him, and you gave an empathic response. Kitty, stop beating up on yourself. You are doing a good job, and it is tough being a single parent. I think Sean was crying because he was missing his father as well as feeling sad because of the punishment which, to a child, suggests that someone is angry with him and with his behavior.

You are providing structure for Sean; I do not think it sounds like you are being dictatorial. It sounds like a parent helping a child to understand the rules. Parents get cross and angry, just like children sometimes become cross and angry. Parents are people who have moods and emotions. We as parents are not always right. We make mistakes too.

You write that Rick "doesn't discipline the kids the way I do," and you think he gets less stressed with them. Rick is functioning in the only way he knows. You are helping him to develop as a responsible adult and parent. Okay, so Rick's personality is different from yours. After all, you are different people. You are not subjecting Sean to an awful torment of being with you. As you told him, the rules at your house are different than the rules at his dad's. You can tell him that it is sometimes difficult adjusting to different rules. But you know he can do this. At school there are different rules, at Dad's house there are different rules than at your house. We learn to adjust to new and different things. It is hard, but it is something we can learn to do and we do it. Praise him and Janie for the adjustment they are making.

Your sister is correct. Sean may not be able to articulate his feelings so he does it by talking about the TV, chair, etc.

Sorry it took me so long to write a more complete answer. Merry Christmas. I hope the holidays are enjoyable for you. I wish you a peaceful 2006.

Fondly,

There are important things to remember and understand when telling children about an impending divorce. Several factors affect the child's adjustment to a divorce: how the child is told; the well-being of the parent with whom the child is living; the child's relationship to both parents before the breakup; both the parents' and child's ability to deal with stress; and the availability of a support system.

Unless there is violence or abuse, children will want to maintain as good a relationship with both their parents as possible. Children feel shocked, bewildered, and lonely when they hear the news that their parents are separating or divorcing. Most children would prefer their parents' marriage to continue, although most have at times considered the marriage to have been unhappy.

Research tells us that five to six years after a divorce, only a small number of children think that their parents were wrong to have divorced. At the time of the divorce, however, children usually do not understand why their parents have spilt up. Children feel sad and anxious at the possibility of losing touch with the parent who is leaving. When there is a separation prior to a divorce, children are confused because they do not know whether the separation is temporary or permanent. This threatens a child's sense of security. Many children fantasize about their parents getting back together—even after long periods of separation. However little the parents may know of the future, the children know even less. Children and parents give strikingly different pictures of their feelings and of their understanding of the reasons for separation. All children will feel upset, even if they do not say so and even if they do not show it.

GOLDEN RULES

1. Tell your children why (if appropriate) you are divorcing. Give them a reason that is easy to understand. Try to tell them when the whole family (including both spouses and all children) is together.
2. Be available to listen.
3. Reassure your children that the divorce is not their fault.
4. Tell the truth to your children so as not to fuel expectations about a possible reunion. Gently remind children that the divorce is final and that you will not get back together. If children are to learn to trust, the truth must always be told. Every time children are told an untruth, we carve away at their ability to trust.
5. Do not dismiss children's perceptions of events, because this can cause children to doubt their own observations and judgments.
6. Do not provide too many details that will overwhelm the children.
7. Don't hide your emotions. Children should know you feel sad over the loss. It gives children permission to express their sadness. Never say "Don't feel scared or sad."
8. Use age-appropriate language.
9. Remind children that both parents love them.
10. Encourage discussions with children about their thoughts and feelings; be sensitive to children's fears.

11. Use a calendar to show young children when they will see the noncustodial parent. Very young children have little concept of time. Reassuring children that they will see the parent "next Sunday" has little meaning for them, but showing the days on a calendar can help.
12. Transitional objects are useful for young children. Following a divorce or separation, young children may be fearful of abandonment. A transitional object, such as a favorite teddy bear or blanket, can offer comfort and be reassuring to the child.
13. Avoid drama. Talk to the children when you are calm.
14. Try to keep conversations neutral and nonblaming.
15. Be patient.
16. Try to limit the damage caused by divorce.

Three

Moving Out and the Emotional Reaction of Children

Every tomorrow has two handles.
We can take hold of it by the handle of anxiety
or by the handle of faith.

—Unknown

Once the decision has been made to live apart, the couple needs to devise a plan for the separation. Who moves out? When? How will it be accomplished? The logistics of the separation need to be worked out ahead of time so that a unified plan is presented to the children—one that is straightforward and not confusing. It is very important for children to know where the other parent is moving. Having a concrete picture of where the parent lives is soothing. In an ideal world, it would benefit everyone in the family if the couple jointly decided on the relocation place. Preferably, for the sake of the children, the house would be within walking distance or a few minutes away from the other parent. Within a short period of time, a visit to the new residence would be beneficial. Seeing the parent's new home allays anxiety about the well-being of the parent and also helps the children deal with their own separation anxiety.

Sometimes, in an adversarial relationship, none of the above occurs, which is obviously difficult for children. A common reality is that one of the parents abruptly walks out or just disappears. This unfortunate situation is typified by the cliché of the parent who goes out to the corner store and never comes back.

Often children have been aware of discord, arguments, and fights, and so it would seemingly come as no surprise when they are told that the parents are separating. But when confronted with the reality of a parent moving out, they are usually upset despite the relief they may feel about the cessation of all the hostility.

As can be seen from the following two letters and responses, moving out raises many problems and is upsetting for all children. It brings up issues such as anxiety over the separation, guilt, anger at the loss, and frustration.

Hi Dr. L.,

I am still a little bothered by Janie's anger, but we're working on it.

But now I have another question. What should I do with the kids on the day Rick moves out? What should I tell them about staying over at his house? Do you have any thoughts on how to plan what they take to their dad's house? I don't think they understand that it's another home; rather, in their heads, I think it's more of a case of "I'll take this book and this doll."

I really appreciate your taking time out to write me and help with the kids.

Thanks,
Kitty

Hi Kitty,

Your instincts are correct. Seeing Rick moving his things out of the house will affect them. Absolutely, take them out of the house while the moving is going on. Neither you nor the children need to sit and watch while this is taking place. As you have done, prepare Janie and Sean that Daddy is moving his special things to his new house and that they will visit him and stay overnight at his new house, and you will pick them up on Sunday. Give an exact time and make sure you are there exactly on time. Do not cause any stress or anxiety by being late. Perhaps you might consider calling them as you are leaving to pick them up, "I am leaving our house now and will be at Dad's in minutes."

Suggestion: get a calendar on which you mark the days they are with you and the days they are at Rick's house, days of sleepovers, and other important dates. The calendar should be in a prominent place so they are aware of what will be happening and when. Anticipation is very important. No surprises. Explain that you will be working when they stay overnight with Rick. Give Janie your phone number so that she can call if need be, and she will trust that you are where you say you are.

Tell both of them that you understand this is an upsetting situation for them, and it is okay to talk about their feelings. Everybody shows their feelings in different ways. One way is not better than another, they are just different.

If Janie cries, ask her to help you understand why she is crying. Just be gentle and sympathetic with her. Sean and Janie may act out their feelings at school because they are transferring feelings from the separation onto the new school situation. You can give that interpretation. Of course, this hypothesis may be met with "that's not so." It's okay, because they do not have to agree with the interpretation even though it might be true.

Hope I answered everything. Keep calm and explain and anticipate.

Fondly,

Hi Dr. L.,

I have been thinking of you, thinking that I would like to thank you for your help with Janie and to ask your advice for the next few weeks.

The kids and I went with Mum and Dad on a holiday at the beginning of July, and it seemed that taking her out of the situation at home did the trick. She told me all the time that she loved me—like every hour or so—and I told her I loved her too, and on different occasions that it wasn't her fault that Rick and I were splitting up. She was so calm then, and, since then, she's been almost a different child. She can control her temper better—but I'm dealing with her better too, you know? I'm not as stressed when she gets into a temper, and so the whole situation is much calmer, and we avoid escalation. Rick will move out and into his new house on Saturday, September 3.

What I plan to do is to take the kids away first thing on Saturday so they don't see Rick taking his things out (Rick says that it won't affect them if they see this!), and then I'll bring them to him on Saturday evening. He has them until Sunday teatime, and then I'll collect them and have them Sunday night. I'm working the Monday and Tuesday night shift, so Rick will have the kids Monday and Tuesday nights all the time and then either a Friday teatime until Saturday teatime, or a Saturday teatime until Sunday teatime. I may be getting another job, still night shift, but different nights each week, so we'll have to rearrange the kids' time then. But for now, things are going okay. The good thing, for me, is that the weekday nights Rick has the kids, I'll be working, and they are used to me being away all night then. Janie keeps saying to me, "I'll miss Daddy when he's away," and then she might say, "I'll miss you when I'm with Daddy," but not very often.

When I told her the date Rick was moving, she stayed very quiet for a few hours. I'm just concerned that I don't know how to make his going

> easy/less awful for both her and Sean. I mean, I'm relieved that he's going, and I just want to make the house mine, but I suppose I'm wary of how the kids are going to react. Sean will be different, probably whinier. He's going into a new class this year—a new teacher, and he was very close to his previous teacher, so that's going to be a difficult transition for him anyway. Janie has the tendencies to act out and cry, so I don't know. I just don't feel prepared to prepare her, if you know what I mean. I'd like to be able to give her the tools to at least begin to cope with what's going to happen. I really appreciate the time and concern you're giving me and look forward to hearing from you again. Keep well,
>
> Thanks,
> Kitty

Children do not have to be subjected to the anguish of watching a parent pack their belongings, nor to the parents' emotions while doing so. Their emotions do not need to be manipulated and exploited by this disturbing event. To witness the drama of a parent's departure is a scene that might haunt a child for the rest of his or her life. It is a parent's job to take care of a child. It is not a child's job to take care of the parent.

The following excerpt captures a child's anguish at watching his father pack his belongings before moving out.

> The scene is frozen in my mind. I can see my dad standing at the armoire throwing his socks and underwear into a suitcase. I remember watching him pack many times before for business trips. But this was different. I knew he was leaving our house forever. He shouldn't have said to me, "Come and keep me company, Scottie." It was a thoughtless and cruel thing to do. As the anxiety mounted in me, I remember pleading and crying to him, "Daddy, please don't leave, please don't leave."

EMOTIONAL REACTIONS TO DIVORCE

The number of children with mental health problems is on the rise. As parents, we assume we know what is best for our children. As loving parents, we claim that we would never do anything to place our children in a situation that will make them unhappy or bring emotional disorder into their lives. Yet statistics show that 1 in 10 children between 1 and 15 years old have a mental health problem.[1] These include anxieties, phobias, and depression, with symptoms ranging from trouble sleeping to temper tantrums.

A child, feeling the effects of a parent's separation and divorce, may show signs of separation anxiety, depression, phobias, sleep difficulties, isolation, and agitation. Regression may be observed in younger children. Thumb-sucking, bed-wetting, language deterioration, and nightmares may be observed. Older children may demonstrate their distress by a decline in their academic performance, angry outbursts, use of alcohol or drugs, or recklessness.

As described in the following letter, Claudette, age seven, had a tantrum every morning before going to school, fearing the impending separation from her mother. She had already lost her father and could not risk losing her mother as well.

Dr. L.,

I am at my wit's end! Claudette's tantrums have not abated since Steve and I separated. Each morning before school she goes through a ritual of asking me what time I will pick her up from school, where will I be standing as I wait for her, what time I will arrive at the school, and whether I will be there when the bell rings to let the children out. Every answer I give is not good enough. She has a negative scenario ready for each answer that I give.

Jeanne

Dear Jeanne,

I think Claudette is reacting to the separation between you and Steve. She feels uncertain and anxious about everything.

Because Claudette feels everything has gone so wrong in her life, her parents no longer living together, she makes the assumption that everything will continue to be negative and so negates all of the scenarios you present to her.

For a while, you will have to patiently reassure her that you will be there to pick her up after school.

Regards,

In an interview on National Public Radio, James Prosek discussed his book *The Day My Mother Left*. The book is largely autobiographical, although it is billed as fiction. It follows the life of a nine-year-old boy as his parents go through a bitter divorce. The mother abandons the family without saying good-bye. The boy then finds solace in the woods, sketching the wildlife he encounters. Prosek, a critically acclaimed author and wildlife artist, said the experience of being abandoned by his mother helped him discover nature and his gifts for art.

Here a 30-year-old woman remembers how she was told of her parents' impending divorce and that her father would be moving out.

> I woke up to the sound of the front door bell ringing and ringing and ringing. "Who could that be?" I thought. Then I heard the fighting starting again. I thought, "They are at it again." I did not think much more of it—they were always fighting—until I went downstairs. My mom was fidgeting at the stove, and there was a silence that did not feel right. Then my mom blurted out, "We are getting divorced. I am not going to live unhappy for your sake. I know this is going to deeply hurt you, but I would be hurt otherwise. Your dad is moving out today." I realized at that point that I wanted my mother to be happy, even though it would be hard for me to live two lives. My world, which had once been Technicolor, turned and now was stark black and white.

A 22-year-old woman recalls how her parents told her and her sister that they planned to separate and that their father was going to move away. She was six years old at the time; her sister was four.

> I remember everything. I remember it was a Sunday. Dad was actually home and I was sick. They woke us up and brought us down to the kitchen table. Dad brought in a box of Kleenex and put it on the table.
>
> Dad explained he was going to move away. Mom and Dad would not live together anymore. I asked, "Do you still love each other?" They looked at each other; everybody was crying. We had this huge garbage can made of this woven material; the Kleenex was just piled into it and was spilling out over the top. I was just crying and not understanding it. I just knew Dad was leaving. I kept asking questions—"Why is this happening? You don't argue? You still kiss each other." Shocking to a child. It did not make sense. He was never around a lot. I remember I was excited to start kindergarten because then I would get to see him before he went to work.
>
> After they told us, it was just like a normal Sunday. The next week, he moved out. He moved in with my uncle—he really wasn't my uncle, we just called him that; he was real cool. He lived about 15 minutes away. There was a pool and a waterbed. We would jump up and down on the waterbed.
>
> It was almost better when he moved out, because now we got to see him more than when he lived at the house.
>
> I do not remember being upset until they began to date each other again, three years later. When they began to date again, we would have Family Fun Night. We went to look at new big houses—we were all excited. All of a sudden it did not happen. I felt confused. No more Family Fun Nights, no explanations. It went back to the way it was before. It was fine again. Them being apart seemed more normal.

> I asked my mother when I was 15 years old why they got divorced. She explained that Dad was working so much she thought he was not devoting enough time to having a family. Then Mom assumed he was having an affair. "That was the last straw." He had become a top executive. She was not social. He wanted that lifestyle; she did not.

Alexandra, now a divorced mother with children of her own, reflecting on her father's moving out, said:

> I don't actually remember my dad moving out. My parents had separated several times before the final separation and divorce. So the memories are all blurred together. I do, however, remember many moves that were upsetting. After the final separation and before the divorce, we were sent to summer camp. We returned to find that my mother had sold our house and bought a new one in a different neighborhood, which meant we had lost all of our school and neighborhood friends. We had no preparation for this. We now had to go to a new school, make new friends, and acquaint ourselves with a new neighborhood. Three years later, she moved us again. This time the move was even harder. My mother was remarried, and my stepfather was a professor at a prestigious East Coast university. We moved from a house on the West Coast replete with a garden, sunshine, and flowers, to a somewhat dark, though big, apartment in an intellectual, urban neighborhood. We now had to go to a very different kind of school attached to the university. There were even kids whose fathers were Nobel laureates. It was a culture shock.
>
> My sister Anastasia had the hardest time of all of us. When we moved cross-country, she was just entering adolescence. She was the one who was most attached to our father. She had the most friends. She was the "it" girl in her class. She was very popular. The uprooting was very difficult for her. It was probably hard for my brother as well. He was about 11 at the time and never really found his place. He is kind of a lost soul, and I wonder if it relates to the divorce and the various moves.

A parent's moving out of the house brings a sense of reality to what is about to occur: the parents' separation and divorce. These letters demonstrate how a move can disrupt, traumatize, and change a child's perspective on the world. An awareness of the child's feelings and talking to the child can prevent these difficulties.

GOLDEN RULES

1. Talk about the move or the splitting up of the household.
2. Help the children anticipate the change.
3. Maintain relationships and routines. Consistency and stability are of paramount importance. Time spent with each parent has changed. Emotions are in turmoil, and living arrangements are initially confusing, so it is vital that as much constancy as possible be maintained. Preserve as many routines of your child's former life as possible. Keep up relationships with grandparents, aunts and uncles, neighbors, and friends.
4. Stay calm on moving day.
5. Children should not witness the actual moving out.
6. Be aware that children are particularly emotionally vulnerable at this time.
7. Pay attention to the moods of your children.
8. When a parent moves out of the family home, the children may appear to be unaffected; however, there is always an underlying emotional reaction.
9. Monitor your own behavior carefully. Try to shield your children from your stress.
10. Try to minimize the changes that divorce brings. For example, try to keep children in the same school, the same home, and involved in the same activities.

Four

Custody

> In that way King Solomon in his wisdom knew that she was the real mother. A real mother does not cut the child in half.
>
> —1 Kings 3

A REAL MOTHER DOES NOT CUT THE CHILD IN HALF

In the Old Testament, King Solomon is approached by two women, each claiming to be the real mother of an infant. The two women protested, haggled, and were adamant over the maternity of the child. Finally, King Solomon called for a sword and proposed dividing the child in two, giving half to each woman. With that, one of the women screamed, "O my lord, give her the living child, and in no wise slay it." The other woman said, "Let it be neither mine nor thine, but divide it." Knowing that the real mother would never consent to having her child cut in half, he determined that the first woman was the child's mother.

Divorce is difficult and upsetting and can become especially disturbing when custody becomes an issue between divorcing partners. Parents may feel a dilemma very similar to King Solomon's. Historically, most divorce laws have been established through state statutes, and there is variance from state to state. There is, however, one common feature: the best interest of the children is the main priority in all court custody negotiations. Additionally, mediation is often considered as a viable alternative for custody decisions and may replace some of the court's active involvement in determining a custody decision.

With the welfare of the child in mind, two types of custody have been established within the family law system: legal custody and physical custody. Legal sole custody grants one parent exclusive discretion in making major decisions that will affect the child's life. These decisions concern health care, child care, education, extracurricular activities, religion, and other important aspects of the child's life. Parents may share physical custody, or one parent may have sole legal custody.

Physical custody determines with whom the children will live and spend the majority of their time. The three basic residential arrangements include primary mother, primary father, and dual residence. Sole physical custody occurs when the child lives with the legal custodial parent, and the other parent has no custody rights. Seventy percent of all child custody cases name the mother as the custodial parent; the father is named as sole custodian less than 10 percent of the time; and shared custody is awarded in approximately 20 percent of all divorces.[1]

Shared custody means both parents share legal and physical custody of the children. In most shared custody cases, a mediator assists the parents in coming up with a parenting plan. In order to be enforceable, a parenting plan must be written and signed by both parents and a judge.

Joint physical custody refers to the situation where the children live with both parents. It may also occur when both parents make a decision that the children live with only one parent. In joint custody cases, one parent may have primary custody and the other parent is given child visitation rights. This allows the noncustodial parent to take physical custody of the child at specific times such as every other weekend or for certain holidays.

It has become more common for the courts to award some sort of shared custody arrangements to allow both parents to equally participate in the child's life. Shared custody is more common in higher socioeconomic groups and tends to occur more often with older children. Sometimes the custody decision is based on gender: boys will be placed with their father, girls with their mother. Sole custody is usually granted only in circumstances when one parent poses a potential threat to the child's welfare. These dangers can include a history of violence and destructive behavior, and/or alcohol or drug abuse, threats of kidnapping, a history of placing the child in dangerous situations, or psychological abuse. When a parent is denied custody on the above grounds, the court may award child visitation that is supervised by a neutral third-party adult.

Custody is never granted on a permanent basis and can be modified at the discretion of the family court. When parents are unable to settle child custody arguments, the court will intercede. Mediation typically is used to work out such conflicts. Custody disputes are often a product of the divorcing couple's anger at each other. Financial considerations often contribute to custody disputes.

The amount of child support is determined by the court and is based on a predetermined formula. A positive relationship has been found between the payment of child support and shared custody. In a shared custody arrangement, each parent pays for part of the child's fixed and nonfixed expenses.

Child support guidelines stipulate that, the more children in the family, the less amount of support devoted to each child. This guideline is based on the recognition that the amount needed to support two children is less than twice the amount needed to support one child, because you do not need two kitchens or two living rooms for two children. However, with shared physical custody, the child support formula is more difficult to determine, and it is in such cases that bitter child support battles tend to be fought. Parents may begin to fight about ancillary issues and may reopen the physical custody battle as a ploy to avoid the financial obligations. The parent who has physical custody may become intimidated and fearful of losing physical custody and so give in rather than fight.

In instances in which there is a history of domestic violence in the home, courts often order supervised visitation. In this type of visitation, a third party oversees the transfer of the children between parents, and they monitor the visit. This creates opportunities for children to have a safe and conflict-free visit with the noncustodial parent. Supervised visitation is ordered when there are allegations against the noncustodial parent of:

- domestic abuse
- drug or alcohol abuse
- sexual abuse
- physical abuse
- abduction
- long absenteeism

There are three types of supervised visitation:

- Supervised visitation with a professionally authorized provider—for example, a social worker at a supervised center—or supervised visitation with a family member or nonprofessional provider.
- Supervision of the exchange of child between the parents by, for example, a neutral third party.
- Court-ordered therapeutic intervention visitation by a professional, when the parent has been convicted of domestic violence against the children or convicted of a child abuse statute.

Supervised visitation ensures that both parents have access to the child in a safe and secure environment following the divorce. Nancy Fallows, executive director of Supervised Visitation Network, a Tennessee-based association for nonprofit providers, states, "Courts have a growing awareness that it might not be appropriate to leave a child alone" with a parent who has displayed certain behaviors. "Yet, protecting and nurturing that relationship is very valuable to the child."[2] It is the hope that this type of visitation reduces conflict for families.

There is no public funding for supervised visitation; parents must pay the cost. In some cases, the noncustodial parent is unable to afford the cost of supervised visitation, and an insurmountable difficulty is created. A parent may go months without seeing the child because he or she is unable to absorb the cost of the supervised visitation.

Many states have free supervision conducted through nonprofit agencies, but often there are long waiting lists for these services and they have limited resources, which permit supervision for a restricted time. Parents who lose the ability to participate in these programs may lose access to their children, potentially leaving both the children and the parent bereft.

CUSTODY AND MALICE

Divorce can be extremely painful for children, and a continuous custody battle increases the trauma dramatically. Rosie, now 25 years old, was 5 when her parents divorced. It was a bitter and vicious custody battle. Rosie, an only child, was used as a pawn between the battling adults.

> It was all so confusing. I still do not understand parts of it. My dad has a lot of money and would buy me these designer outfits, which I was only allowed to wear at his house. There was this one little dress that I begged him to allow me to take home so I could wear it to my friend Isabelle's birthday party, but he would never permit it. He would tell me no, the dress needed to be kept safe and clean at his house. In fact, in order to stick it to my mom, he would return me to my mom's house in one of the "special outfits" and in the apartment hallway he would take off all my clothes, leaving me in my undershirt and panties while he took his "good clothes" away. He would knock on the door, and my mother would have to bring me "her clothes." It was humiliating and very upsetting. On one occasion, he kidnapped me. He told me I would be staying with him now. I know my mom called and called, and he never answered the phone. Finally, the police arrived at the door. What he didn't realize was that his behavior caused me to distrust and dislike him rather than endear him to me. I never wanted to visit him, and even now I see him as seldom as possible.

Sometimes children are used as vehicle to inflict pain on the ex-spouse. Examples of this include accusations of child molestation, reporting untrue allegations of child endangerment to the authorities, and murder. The *Seattle*

Post-Intelligencer reported the following horrifying story in March 2007. Eric Johnson had not wanted a divorce. He had threatened his wife with a gun, had moved out under police supervision, and was "very bitter about the divorce." He wanted custody of his daughter.

> "I've got her, and you're not going to get her." Beth Johnson heard those words from her ex-husband Monday, shortly before he crashed his rented single-engine plane into his former mother-in-law's southern Indiana home, killing himself and the couple's eight-year-old daughter. "That was the only way he could hurt Beth," said the child's grandmother. The police felt that the crash was intentional and deliberate. A phone call was made prior to the crash and the child was heard saying "Mommy come get me, Mommy come get me."[3]

CHILDREN'S TESTIMONY IN CHILD CUSTODY BATTLES

Children almost always are better off when both parents remain actively involved in their lives. Both parents may love their children and want what is best for the children, but, when custody issues are being established, the welfare of the child is often temporarily put aside. Bitter custody battles can last for years, and the residual effect on the child can last a lifetime. Children are put in the untenable situation of essentially having to choose one parent over another, thus suffering terrible conflicts around loyalty and feelings of betrayal. They may be encouraged to fabricate stories or even support one parent's outright lies.

Theo remembers the bitter custody battle between his parents; he felt torn, confused, and guilty. His mother had been hospitalized for depression when he was five years old. There was a prolonged custody battle between his parents, and he felt he was forced to testify against his mother. He was asked to describe his mother's behavior before her hospitalization. When he said he did not remember, he was asked leading questions that led to his father winning custody, something for which he now feels responsible. When he spoke with the judge in private, he was assured that what he told the judge would be held in strict confidence—it would be "a secret." He remembers his mother weeping when his father was awarded custody and saying to him, "How could you tell the judge that I slept all the time and never paid attention to you? I was sick then, but now I am better." He felt betrayed by the judge's revealing their "secret" conversation and was distraught at his mother's pain and his own "encouraged" disloyalty.

> I was only five, had no ability to recognize how damning my words would be. They asked me, "Does your mom sleep a lot during the day?" and I said yes, with no recognition of what they were trying to prove. Of course, now

I realize it only had to do with money. After the hospitalization, my mom was fully functional, but Dad did not want to pay her child support. I am not sure my welfare was the real issue.

"MUSICAL CHAIRS" CUSTODY

Traditionally, mothers were awarded physical custody, and fathers were granted visitation rights. However, this traditional arrangement has changed much in recent decades. With societal changes, men began seeking physical custody of their children. They no longer were satisfied with being the "weekend" father. They wanted to be full participants in the raising of their children. With this movement, joint custody and shared physical custody became prevalent. Rather than the traditional arrangement of children living full time with one parent, a child might spend three days a week with one parent and the remaining part of the week with the other parent. Another variation could be one week with one parent, one week with the other—or even one month with one parent, one month with the other. This arrangement is often very difficult for children.

The following three letters describe the progression of a shared physical custody arrangement from the child's point of view.

Hi Dr. L.,

I feel so badly that I screwed up and missed my appointment. Don't take it personally, I screwed up with everyone! I missed a dentist appointment, I left my project at my dad's house, I was late for school, and I messed up everywhere.

I guess it is part of this thing of being at one house for three days and then, just like musical chairs, changing again. I never know which end is up. My grades are slipping because I am always forgetting homework or books or something at one of the houses. My teachers are frustrated with me, and it's not even really my fault. Even my friends are complaining that they never know where to come and get me, my dad's or my mom's. I hardly know myself! Oh yeah, I left my tights, the orange ones that I like to wear with my black skirt at my dad's. So I had to wear black tights with the black skirt and went to the party looking like a nerd!

Emma

Hi Emma,

Musical chairs are a difficult game and an impossible situation. I will see you next week, and we will talk about strategies. I'm sure you looked great at the party and not at all nerd-like.

Hi Dr. L.,

Thanksgiving in Florida is quite a trip! I'm so glad my grandmother retired here. It's hot! I even went swimming this morning while all of you in Chicago are freezing.

I wanted to wish you a happy Thanksgiving but also wanted to tell you what I have been thinking about. Things are much better now that I am not doing the musical chairs every three days. Changing houses every month is so much easier and better. But what do you think? Do you think I could live with just with one of them all of the time? I don't want to hurt either one of their feelings but am sick of being a volleyball. I'd really like to live with my dad because he lives close to my school, and my two best friends live on the next block. My mom would be crushed and think I don't love her, but I'm just a kid that wants to be close to the action. Watch'a think?

Emma

Dear Emma,

Happy Thanksgiving. Swimming sounds wonderful and, yes, Chicago's pretty cold right now!

This is a subject that needs serious thought. It's a real dilemma. We need to explore this fully. It's not something that can be decided quickly, and we will begin to talk about it when you return from Florida.

Regards,

Dr. L.,

I'm so hyped. Thing are going really well. I just wanted to let you know before I see you again. I love living with my dad, and my mom has been pretty cool about it. I feel like I am part of the crowd again—Jenny is always at my house or I'm at her house. It is super!

My mom and I are planning a great vacation in the summer.

See ya Tuesday
XXXXXXXXX
Emma

In Emma's situation, both parents were reasonable and focused on her best interest, and a compromise was reached with which everyone could live.

Not all situations are resolved as well. In an article that appeared in the *New York Times*, Stephen Perrine succinctly describes the pain of being the noncustodial parent.[4] He bemoans that four and a half years after his divorce, he only sees his two adolescent daughters every other weekend. As his daughters' school schedules permit, he skis and plays tennis with them. "We're all keenly aware of the thin membrane of secrecy that keeps us from being as close as we were before their mom and I divorced." Perrine laments that his daughters, "whom I've loved for a decade and a half, seem like little strangers to me." He regrets that he is not part of their daily life and that the girls do not "tell me some detail of their lives—or downright lie if they have to—so I won't feel sad that I've missed something they shared with their mom, or raise issue over some decision she's made with which I might not agree." Feeling marginalized, he "sometimes come[s] away from visits or phone calls feeling shaken, saddened and angry."[5] Such situations evoke enormous sympathy. However, the child's emotional well-being should be the primary concern, despite a parent's own needs, no matter how difficult it is for the parent.

CUSTODY SECRETS AND LIES

In this section, a husband describes the effect of secrets on a divorce and custody situation.

> She was perfect, beautiful, sweet, and fun. However, soon after we married, she seemed to change. Gone was the sweet façade. After our first child was born, I had to constantly intervene because of her uncontrollable rage and anger at the baby. The rages continued for years. I finally divorced her after I discovered major indiscretions. By this time we had three children, and I was concerned about them. She has a vile and uncontrollable temper, flies into rages at the children, and even hits them in public. The school called me to report her physical abuse of the kids, and I became aware that she was having inappropriate people watch the children until she came home from work. I later found out that she was hospitalized as an adolescent, a secret that she had never revealed.
>
> Initially, I did not seek custody. However, after the school called and after consulting a child psychologist, I realized the children were not safe with her. It was then that I decided to file for custody. I won.

SPLITTING UP CHILDREN IN CUSTODY ARRANGEMENTS

Splitting up children, where one child is placed with the father and one with the mother, is usually not in the best interest of the children. Siblings need each other for support during any difficult time. They may misinterpret and feel hurt by how the decisions were reached to divide them. For example, children who go to live with their father may think the mother does not love them as much. Similarly, children who live with the mother may feel rejected by the father. At the very time that children need the support of their siblings, they are thrust into a competitive and confusing situation with their brother or sister.

Jhumpa and Ashima are both in their late twenties. It is only now, after 15 years living apart, that they are beginning to renegotiate a sisterly relationship. At the time of their parents' divorce, Jhumpa went to live with their father, while Ashima remained with their mother. In this Indian family, the father was a physician who was assimilated into U.S. culture, while the mother retained a traditional Indian lifestyle, surrounded by Indian neighbors and friends.

The girls had been close growing up, but at the time of the divorce, the father, having finished his residency, relocated to another city with Jhumpa. The girls saw each other from time to time but over the years drifted further and further apart.

Jhumpa: "It is as if we come from two different families, two different cultures. My sister knows and practices all the Hindu traditions. She knows the customs, and the meanings of things, and, of course, she is a fabulous exotic cook. I grew up with macaroni and cheese and burgers. I am forever asking, "What's that?" when she presents another Indian dish. We are trying to get to know each other and accept each other's differences, which are vast."

Ashima: "I find her rejection of our culture confusing and a little disloyal. I don't want to be thought of as exotic. I don't like her attitude toward our mother's way of thinking and even her homeopathic remedies. I find it dismissive."

It is as if the two sisters grew up divided by an ocean.

CUSTODY WITH ADOLESCENTS

Sometimes when the children reach adolescence, changes are made in the physical custody arrangement. For instance, boys may go and live with their fathers, seeking male camaraderie and understanding. Or an adolescent may become too difficult for one parent to handle and the other is called upon to help. The result may be that the child is shuttled between the two households; if not handled well, the adolescent may be severely affected.

Visitation schedules can be difficult for youngsters and may become more so as they approach adolescence. Weekends are usually filled with events and activities with friends, sports, trips to the mall, movies, parties, or just "hanging out." Older children can feel deprived and resentful when they have to drop everything for legislated visits. Ideally, parents should try to be flexible with visitation, keeping in mind the child's needs and desires.

Libby, age 16, feels frustrated and torn.

I am close to my dad and I like spending time with him, and I would never do anything to hurt him. I know that he is still reeling from the divorce, and my weekends with him are really important to him. But I really, really want to spend time with my friends. During the week, we are all busy with homework and extracurric's. The weekends are the only time we have to go to the movies or check out the cute boys at the mall. Often there is a party I have to miss because my dad lives far away from my neighborhood. What do I do? Hurt him? Lose out? It's a no-win all the way around. No one in my group has to deal with this mess.

REMARRIAGE AND CUSTODY

When a parent remarries, a child may want to go and live with the other parent because the child may feel angry at, rejected by, or uncomfortable with the new spouse. These decisions need to be thought through very carefully and not made precipitously.

Take, for example, the following case. Bruce was eight when his mother remarried. He was uncomfortable in the household and with his stepfather. Two years later, he asked to live with his father, who was residing on the opposite coast. He went to live with his father for several years. Upon hearing that his mother was in the process of divorcing his stepfather, he announced that he now wanted to live with his mother again. Living with his father in what initially seemed like an ideal situation to Bruce was in reality fraught with difficulties. He had had to completely readjust to a new school, new friends, new rules, new socioeconomic conditions, and regional differences.

ILLNESS AND CUSTODY

This section recounts the impact of personality issues on custody decisions told from a father's point of view.

Scott, a successful internist, was divorced after a 17-year marriage. The problems in his marriage were complex and involved both his homosexuality and his wife Stephanie's destructive behavior. When he first met Stephanie, she "was good-looking, fun to be with, and we enjoyed each other's company immensely. And, to my relief, she wasn't interested in sex before marriage." They married when Scott was 23, because "Stephanie wanted to get married and I got swept up into the vortex. I thought I was cured. I thought marriage is what you did for show, it didn't limit you, and we would make it through."

The first few years of the marriage were reasonably good, despite the fact that Stephanie was "always a rollercoaster, a manic depressive." Scott, immersed in his training and then, later, in building a practice and working long hours, focused on his career and, for the most part, turned a blind eye to their problems. A daughter, Jamie, was born. When Jamie was four, the problems in the marriage exploded. Stephanie voiced her concerns regarding their sexual relationship. It was at this point that Scott decided it was unfair to have her question herself, and so he told her of his homosexual preference. "Her reaction was to become hysterical and pick a fight with my parents!" She talked of moving back to her parents on the West Coast and taking Jamie with her.

"Initially I was relieved yet became overwhelmed as I realized I, as a young professional, would have to be responsible for providing for two households and would have to deal with a divorce long-distance." The situation eventually defused, and nothing more was said. The marriage became increasingly unhappy and frustrating to both parties but continued. Four years after their daughter's birth, a son, Tom, was born.

When Tom was 8 years old and Jamie was 12, Stephanie accosted Scott over finances, "became hysterical," and informed Scott she was filing for divorce. She had entered the workforce, felt more secure, and was cognizant of her own attractiveness and desirability.

Scott chose to pursue custody in order to protect the children from their mother's "chaotic" behavior, her constant denigration and devaluation of them, her dogmatic need to control (sometimes forcing them to eat within a certain amount of time), her lack of empathy for them, and her putting her needs before theirs. At times, Scott had to physically separate her from the children. She was abusive and destructive. "I was barely 40 years old. I could have lived on half my income and could have begun a new life. But she was horrible to the kids, demeaning them."

During the divorce and 18-month custody battle, both parents and children continued to live together in their suburban house. The children were spared verbal battles between the parents, and they all continued in their familiar roles. After the parents underwent court-ordered psychiatric evaluations, Scott was awarded custody by the judge. Did the psychiatrists make their recommendations based on Stephanie's volatile moods, on her constant devaluation and denigration of her husband and children? Scott was not sure why the judge ruled in his favor, noting only that it was the 1980s—a time in which it was a rare event for fathers to be awarded custody. "I didn't win; she lost."

Stephanie moved out of the house, first to an apartment in a neighboring suburb and then later to an apartment in the city. The children initially saw their mother, although the visits diminished with time. They seemed unaffected by their physical separation from her. Scott tried to keep a civil relationship with Stephanie for the children's sake. "I never allowed the kids to be torn."

Approximately four years later, Jamie left for college, and Tom, entering high school, decided to go and live with his mother. After a year, he could not tolerate living there any longer and appealed to his father to return.

Both children are now adults, have completed graduate degrees, and live independent lives. They both remain close to their father and get on well with his partner of many years.

The following section, from a mother's point of view, describes the impact of both mental and physical issues on a custody situation.

Kate is a 40-year-old of mother of two who lost custody of her children five years ago. A week after returning home from a six-week psychiatric hospitalization, she left an abusive husband in order to seek refuge and file for divorce.

She tells of feeling fed up with her marriage after years of physical and emotional abuse, and after discovering that her husband was having an affair with her best friend who lived next door. The last straw that precipitated her flight to safety was when her husband "threw an iron table at me the very day I returned from the hospital."

When Kate left the house, she fully intended to return for her children after finding an apartment where they could all live safely.

> My husband had been telling me to get out for almost a year. He told me, "I am taking the house and the kids." I ran away not caring about material possessions. I planned on coming back for my children. After all, the mother always gets the kids, right? There was no doubt in my mind that the children would be with me. I had a file of police and medical records showing my history of being hit and beaten.
>
> After a week, my husband's attorney painted the following picture of me to the judge. "She is bipolar. She is unstable. She is lazy. She can't be a good mother." I was even put on supervised visitation for absolutely no reason at all. Since I was just treated for severe depression the month before I left, the judge decided that I was not stable and might steal the kids.
>
> Here is the truth about what the judge should have been told. Yes, I am bipolar. Aside from being bipolar, I stayed in an emotionally and physically abusive relationship. Anyone would be depressed. I tried everything to make the relationship work. When I found that my husband was sleeping with my best friend in the house next door, I began to feel hopeless and figured the safest place for me was the hospital. It was the safest place. They helped me screw my head on straight. I was ready to leave the marriage when I got out of the hospital.

My leaving was supposed to be a glorious moment of getting away and starting my life over. As you see, everything turned against me. I lost custody because I ran out of money.

Five years later, here I sit with the daily pain of being the only mom who does not have custody. A year after the divorce, I was hospitalized in intensive care and diagnosed with a terrible neurological disease called myasthenia gravis. I went on permanent disability. I now know why I was weak and weary. I was never lazy. I was sick and suffering through the whole marriage and was judged unjustly. Now, after five years, it is nearly impossible for me to get custody of my children. Why? Because there is no evidence of harm by their dad. It is not about how much I could help enrich my children's lives. Now I would have to prove how bad my ex is. No, he is not terrible. I could just add so much more to their lives if they were with me.

I have the ability to be a full-time great mom, but I am not well enough to work to support myself. Being disabled and not working means I have no money. I own nothing and get by on Medicare/Medicaid. I can't afford an attorney. I could show what good I could do for the kids even without saying my ex is doing anything bad, but I am so frightened by the severe lashing out by my ex at our divorce trial that I don't know if I could ever go to court again.

I am frustrated to no end. I cry every day when I look at my kids' empty beds at night. I miss them so much. I think that is a normal maternal instinct. I do have standard visitation, and I make the most of every hour with my children. Many people tell me to fight for what is right. I feel that what is right is not possible. Making things right would require cooperation on my ex-husband's part, and that will never happen.

Is it best to deal with the fact that I cannot change things? If that is the case, how can I cope with the sadness and pain in my heart of missing so much time in my children's lives? No matter what I tell myself, I still cry.

Kate later sent the following email reflecting a new perspective on custody, finance, and the accompanying emotional anguish.

It seems that the conventional way in court is so bad in the long run for the whole family. If there are any other options, people maybe just don't know. Of course, the settlement method depends on the temperament of the divorcing individuals.

Kate

CUSTODY AND HOLIDAYS AND SCHEDULES

A divorce decree usually stipulates holiday and visitation arrangements. These arrangements are not always what the children want and desire. Children often have no voice in the matter and are used as pawns. Quarreling over holiday and weekly visitation and its implementation can cause further conflict for the children, as illustrated in the following letter from Tom, age 12.

Hi Dr. L.,

I am stuck at my uncle's house and it's Christmas. It is so boring. It's just my mom and me and my uncle, his wife, and his twin daughters, who are two years old. Lots of fun! I wish I were with my dad. Christmas with him is always terrific. He has lots of brothers and sisters, and I have lots of cousins my age. There is always something to do. How am I going to get through this long boring day? Dr. L., what can I do? I don't want to go through this again in a couple of years. If I hear my aunt make cutesy sounds to those twins one more time, I am going to scream. This Christmas stinks. I'll never get divorced and do this to my kids.

Hi Tom,

Divorce is hard on kids. But the court decreed that you spend one Christmas with your dad and the next year with your mom. When you are 18, you can decide for yourself where you will spend each Christmas.

I know that divorce is really difficult on kids. Wish I could give you a magical solution. Maybe next time you need to go better prepared with video games, books, and your cell phone.

See you next week.

RELOCATION AND CUSTODY

It is a common occurrence that either the custodial or noncustodial parent moves after divorce. One study showed that, within four years of separation and divorce, about one-fourth of mothers with custody moved to a new location.[6] Another study found that once during childhood children experienced a move of more than one hour's driving distance between their two parents' homes.[7] Among the many reasons for relocating after divorce are a desire to get away from a perceived source of emotional pain, starting over, living closer to sources of emotional support (such as extended family or old friends), and job opportunities.

Joint custody arrangements usually involve lower incidences of relocation by either parent. There are conflicting findings and recommendations on the impact of parental moving and children's welfare after divorce. Some reports encourage both parents to remain in close proximity to their children, whereas other studies conclude that what is good for the custodial parent is good for the child.

In an ideal situation, both parents would live in close proximity to each other after the divorce. A noncustodial parent who lives far away usually makes arrangements to visit the children several times a year. The children then visit that parent during summer vacations and over extended school holidays. This, of course, works best when there is an amicable postdivorce relationship, and the noncustodial parent is interested in staying close to and involved with the children. The absent parent can reinforce the bond and sustain the relationship by making daily phone calls, and the children can be encouraged to do the same.

The following cases and letters illustrate the complexity and ambivalence that sometimes occur with relocation.

Simon, a 40-year-old executive, concerned about his ex-wife's stability and the well-being of his two children, filed for physical custody. The court granted joint custody and awarded him physical custody. The situation worked smoothly for a year. He remarried and was offered an out-of-state career-enhancing position. With his ex-wife's agreement, he purchased a new house in California, and he agreed to purchase her a home nearby so she could continue to live near the children. He only accepted the job with the understanding that his children would be accompanying him. Simon, his new wife, his children, and his ex-wife were all going to move to California.

Simon had begun his new job when he received a letter from his ex-wife's lawyer. She was no longer honoring her agreement and was filing for sole custody of the children. A court battle ensued, and, many thousands of dollars later, Simon found himself hundreds of miles away without his children. The children, who had been living with Simon, were in turmoil. The children had to adjust to their mother's new boyfriend, whom they did not like, and they missed their father and the structure and order that his household provided. Chaos and conflict are not beneficial for children, and Simon's children showed signs of distress both at school and at home.

Polly was nine when her parents divorced. Soon thereafter her father relocated to North Carolina. Each year she would spend either Christmas or Thanksgiving with him.

> I would weep and weep at the airport, begging my mother not to put me on the plane. A few days later I would find myself crying uncontrollably at the Charlotte airport when I was waiting for my flight back to Connecticut.

Dear Dr. L.,

Hi, sorry to bother you, but I have a pressing question that perhaps you can answer for me.

Remember when I wrote to you that I had moved down with my sister to Kentucky? I had told you that the kids really miss their dad, and I feel like I need to move back where he is so that the kids can have two parents. Any thoughts on this?

Thanks,
Debbie

Hi Debbie,

Divorce is complicated, difficult, and painful. The impact on children is particularly tough.

I'll attempt to address the implications of relocation on children after divorce. The first thing that should always be kept in mind is what is in the best interest of the child.

Your children are expressing a need to live closer to their father, and this is completely understandable. This may not be the right choice for you to make considering what you may be giving up to make this happen. In thinking about what is in the best of interest of your children, you must also consider what is best for yourself and ultimately how that will affect your children.

It is your decision to make despite your children's protestations. Nevertheless, this does not mean that your children's feelings should not be understood and heard and discussed. Living far away and not being in close proximity to their dad is not the perfect alternative for your children, but your security and happiness cannot be compromised. Ultimately, you will be a better parent if you feel that your security, both emotional and economic, is protected. Perhaps, should you decide to stay in Kentucky, they could visit their dad more often or perhaps he could visit them regularly?

Hope this helps to answer your question.

Regards,

GOLDEN RULES

1. The best interests of the children are of crucial consideration. Custody fights can be extremely detrimental to both adults and children. Parents are encouraged to try and work out arrangements regarding the children out of court.

2. Try to be reasonable and flexible. Do not react out of anger and spite. The children suffer when this happens.
3. The children's well-being is crucial. Do not use a custody fight to express your anger and bitterness.
4. Remind yourself of the King Solomon story. Children cannot be cut in half; find a workable and fair solution that keeps the children very much intact.
5. Avoid engaging in conflicts. Research concludes that emotional and behavioral problems are more frequent in high-conflict situations.
6. Parents who share custody are encouraged to establish schedules. This gives children a feeling of stability.
7. If you are the parent who pays child support, do not let your children suffer economically by withholding child support.
8. If you are the noncustodial parent, remain involved with your children, seeing them often. Frequency and regularity of visits affect self-esteem and behaviors.
9. Attempt to work out a custody agreement amicably. Custody battles are financially and emotionally costly, and the consequences can be devastating.
10. Make every attempt to keep children with their siblings.

Five

Parental Alienation

Ding dong the wicked Jew is gone.
Now we can eat ham all day long.
—As told to us by the "wicked" father who was a victim of parental alienation

This demeaning ditty illustrates a vindictive mother's denigration of a father following a divorce. Unable to contain her own emotions, the mother sets up the children to be alienated from their father.

The term *parental alienation* first appeared in the work of Dr. Richard Gardner in the 1970s. Parental alienation syndrome occurs in children as a response to conflict between parents, most often in divorce, in which the children ally themselves with one parent and become preoccupied with overly inappropriate criticism of the other parent.

Parental alienation syndrome is the brainwashing of a child by one parent to denigrate, devalue, and alienate the other parent. As part of the syndrome, the child must be coerced into actively shunning the other parent. Parental alienation syndrome is the combination of parental programming with the child's contribution of vilification of the other parent. The severity of parental alienation syndrome is measured by the parent's delusional obsession with the intent and hope of destroying the relationship between the child and the alienated parent. In severe cases, the relationship between child and alienated parent is permanently destroyed.

It is important to clarify what is *not* parental alienation. Some degree of alienation may occur when parents first separate, although it usually diminishes as parents and children adjust to the changes brought on by separation and divorce.

This type of adjustment is not parental alienation. Also, to be considered parental alienation syndrome, the campaign of alienation must be unjustified. When verbal, physical, or sexual abuse causes the child to avoid and alienate the parent, it is not considered parental alienation syndrome.

Parental alienation syndrome is most common after a divorce, particularly when there has been a bitter child custody dispute. However, parental alienation can occur when custody is not an issue. Studies have found that the majority of highly conflicted divorce cases have some characteristics of parental alienation syndrome.

With parental alienation syndrome, the anxiety and anger increase rather than decrease. The alienating parent becomes increasingly and willfully intent on and preoccupied with destroying the relationship between the child and the other parent.

Parental alienation syndrome can be an extremely complicated issue to deal with in divorce and child custody situations because the alienating parent's statements may seem authentic and justified. Situations involving parental alienation syndrome can therefore be difficult to defend in court. To many people, it may seem as if the alienating parent and children are justified in their feelings and behaviors, particularly when false accusations of abuse or mistreatment are made to further a vendetta. A qualified and skilled mental health professional can usually diagnose parental alienation syndrome and testify in court as an expert witness. However, even professionals can err in their diagnosis, particularly when the alienating parent is pathologically skillful and sociopathic.

Cases involving parental alienation syndrome are difficult and complex, and judges may underestimate the magnitude of the problem. An astute and qualified family law attorney who is familiar with and experienced in the area of parental alienation syndrome can be helpful. This legal expert can identify rights and legal options, make sure that interests are protected, and save the children from being placed in an untenable situation.

Because mothers traditionally have custody of the children, parental alienation is usually triggered by the mother's attitudes and behaviors. These behaviors may include:

- Displaying extreme negative behavior toward the father.
- Making demeaning and devaluing statements about the father.
- Inviting the children to ridicule and laugh at the father.
- Subtly suggesting a restriction of communication between the father and children.

- Exhibiting hostile behavior toward the father and encouraging the children to do the same.
- Insisting that the father come and go at specific times and give an exact accounting of how he spends time with the children.
- Changing arrangements and notifying the father at the last minute, sometimes even informing him in a letter that is mailed so late that it cannot possibly reach him on time. She has ultimate control and enjoys using this power.
- Intentionally offering the children enticing alternatives on the days they are scheduled to be with the father and then claiming that it was the children's choice. When the father insists that this is his time, he appears "mean" to the children.
- Intercepting gifts given by the father to the children, breaking or damaging them, "misplacing" a gift before it can be given on the intended day, or duplicating gifts that the father has given to the children so that the children do not value his gifts, or him.
- Deliberately distorting things that the father has said.
- Threatening the father that he will lose contact with the children if he does provide extra child support.
- Failing to keep the father aware of events and happenings in the children's lives.
- Finding any way to criticize and demean the father. This might extend to denigrating the clothes that the father buys for the children.
- Attempting to stop any contact the father has with the children by criticizing his home, his friends, his behavior, and his lifestyle.
- Lying, such as telling the children that the judge said they can only see their dad every two weeks when, in fact, the court may have stipulated a different, more generous visitation schedule.
- Interfering with fun arrangements the father has made by allowing homework to accumulate during the week so that it has to be done when the children are with the father.
- Making it difficult for the father's parents to see their grandchildren.
- Limiting the father's participation with the school and school events by incorrectly informing the school that this is in violation of the divorce agreement.
- If the father is involved in a new relationship, insisting that the new person have nothing to do with the children because it will upset them.

- Tampering with phone calls to the child, saying the child is busy or out or listening in on or interrupting the call.
- Demeaning and provoking the father in front of the children, and, should he attempt to defend himself or retaliate, using his behavior as a threat to bring him back to court.
- Exhibiting emotional problems.

These behaviors on the part of the mother often have serious consequences for the parent-child relationship. The child may suddenly begin to make excuses for not seeing the father or his family; they may say they do not want his gifts. The strategy of isolating him from his children will have been effective.

MOTIVATION OF THE MOTHER

There are many reasons that a mother may behave in this way. She may hate the father and want to use the children as a weapon against him; she may be possessive and competitive and want all the children's love; contact with the father may be difficult for her; or her attitudes may be reinforced by other women who are hostile to men. This may be her way of controlling the father and the children; she may feel threatened by the inequities in finances; she may use the children as a bargaining tool to obtain more money; the mother may feel rivalry toward the new partner of the father and so attempt to prevent the child from seeing the father; the mother may be starting a new involvement and does not want the child to tell the father about her new relationship.

STRATEGIES FOR DEALING WITH PARENTAL ALIENATION

If you are involved in a case of parental alienation, perhaps these lines from Rudyard Kipling's *IF* offer comfort.

If you can keep your head when all about you
Are losing theirs and blaming it on you,
If you can trust yourself when all men doubt you
But make allowance for their doubting too,
If you can wait and not be tired by waiting,
Or being lied about, don't deal in lies,
Or being hated, don't give way to hating,
And yet don't look too good, nor talk too wise:
. . . If you can bear to hear the truth you've spoken
twisted by knaves to make a trap for fools.

Those experiencing parental alienation should keep in mind the following:

- Do not put the child in the middle.
- Be aware that children often are reconciled at a later time.
- It is normal to grieve for the perceived loss of a child.
- Seek support groups and other opportunities to talk about the loss.
- Learn as much about parental alienation as possible.
- Know that you are not alone; this is a common situation.
- Seek out groups for other parents in the same situation.

The following letter is an example of parental alienation syndrome. As outsiders, it is easy for us to see how the boy's relationship with his father has been manipulated by the mother.

Dear Dr. L.,

Just writing to say "hi" from sunny California (ha, ha). Today we had a great day at the beach and we saw a guy who acted just like my dad. He was bald and fat like my dad, a big creep! OOOH, Yuck. And he was bossing everyone around. My mom pointed him out and then we all laughed.

We are having a great time, the only thing is, I'd really like to go ocean fishing. My mom says we can't do that because it is reckless, irresponsible, and dangerous—and besides, it reminds her of my dad. I don't want to be like my dad and be irresponsible and reckless. So instead, we're going to go to the museum—not my first choice, but I guess it will be okay.

I don't miss my dad at all, and we don't need him. Boy, I'm glad I don't live with him.

Write me,
Marc

Hi Marc,

I'm glad you are having a great time. I think you really wanted to go fishing because that was something you did with your dad. Perhaps you do miss him. I know your mom is angry with your dad. You do not have to have the same feelings as your mom. Just because your mom is angry, doesn't mean you have to be angry, too. This is something we can talk more about when you get back.

Regards,

Marc's mother wants to destroy the bond between her children and their father. Any positive association that the children have toward their father is twisted into a negative. This is destructive and unhealthy for the children. As a boy, Marc's identification with his father is crucial for healthy development. The father should be perceived in a positive light in order for the son to develop a healthy self-concept and for him to build a positive male identification. Marc is being manipulated out of his mother's anger. She is willfully attempting to destroy any future relationship with the father. This does not bode well for Marc's future with male teachers, bosses, or other male authority figures—or for his life in general.

Parental alienation can also be disastrous for girls, as seen in the following letter.

> Dad,
>
> I hate you. Pay my mom back for all of the bills that you said you would take care of, but didn't. That saves our house and saves me a lot of stress. It will give my mother a longer life. She doesn't want anything more than that. Neither do I. All I want to do is live a normal life. How can I live a normal life with the promises you make and the lies you feed me? Mom just explained to me that you paid off our house due to a court order. But I also know that Mom never asked you for a penny more in court. She could have but didn't want to create problems.
>
> It is clear that you could have given more, and Mom should have taken you back into court as I got older and my needs increased. Mom took on two jobs, and Miles helped us out. Mom said she had to sell all of her valuables and now there is nothing left for me. I told Mom I hated you, and she said I should hate you because you are rich, cheap, and mean. She said if you loved me you would not behave this way. Miles made it possible for Mom and me to go on vacations together, not you. He made it possible for me to have piano and skating lessons, not you.
>
> I am flunking out in school. I got angry and fresh with my math teacher, who is just like you, and I've been suspended.
>
> I was telling my friend Katie about you. Katie says that's why she hates men, they're all just like you. She's invited me to go to the Gay Club at school; maybe I will.
>
> Miranda

Children usually grow up loving both of their parents. In a bitter divorce, attempted alienation is not uncommon. Negative statements like "You are just like your mother/father" should be avoided. Fury, bitterness, and resentment by one parent toward the parting partner can result in estrangement and alienation.

In the following section, a 24-year-old woman describes the consequences of parental alienation.

When I think of marriage, I am always second-guessing myself because I do not want to end up like my parents.

I do not expect anything from my dad; I am just numb to him. I was five years old when they got divorced. My brothers and sisters were one, two, seven, and nine years old. I never remember being told that they were going to divorce. I just always remember two separate households, ours and his.

We went every other weekend to Dad's house. It was always fun—we did not have to eat healthy meals and we were always going on adventures.

At the age of 13, we got to decide whether we wanted to go to his house or not. Sometimes I wanted to go, other times I did not. But I always felt guilty if I did not go. Mom was probably more of an advocate of us not going. She always said, "Do you know that, at your age, I was already married?" like we're not as mature or grown up as she was.

Mom is always comparing anything and everything to my dad. "You know, you are saying something that your father would say," and that automatically means "I am not happy with you."

Mom came from a very upper-class family. She married someone from the other side of the tracks. She looks at us kids and assumes we will take care of her and support her (her family continues to support her to this day). She tells us she supported us till we got jobs. This is untrue; we all paid for our own educations.

My dad stopped paying child support when were very young. There was a time when the judge put him in jail for not paying child support, and we all went to visit him in jail. He stopped working so he would not have to pay child support. It was at this time that my mom started really denigrating him, saying awful things about him, reminding us of his humble beginnings. She would say things like, "What can you expect from people who are trailer trash." I always wanted to please my mother, so it was at this time that I stopped having anything to do with him. I didn't see him for years.

Before I make my own judgment about someone, usually within a week or so, I have my sisters and mother telling me how to feel. They arrive at a kind of group consensus and decide how I should feel about someone.

The risk of committing to one person for the rest of my life scares me. I have no healthy relationships to compare anything to.

If parents really want to help their children be happy, they have to stop dictating what their children think and say. Good parenting is about permitting children to be themselves. As parents we have to realize that our children are not clones of ourselves and should be permitted to be themselves. We have to teach them to be their own people and allow them to love both of their parents. Independence, courage, and strength should be encouraged.

Occasionally, there are extreme cases of parental alienation. In this letter a 39-year-old woman recounts how she was abducted by her father.

Dear Dr. L.,

Recently I have been reading a novel that takes place in my home town. A bunch of memories from my childhood came to mind, particularly one involving my parents splitting up.

I was nine years old when my parents separated. My father was threatening my mom and her lawyers advised her to "hide out with the kids." Her attorneys kept telling her that he was capable of kidnapping us. My mom felt my dad had a lot of anger issues and thought it was possible that he could do something drastic. In an effort to "protect us," my mom decided to hide us at various relatives' homes. My mom has five brothers and sisters, so we had plenty of choices for our "hideout" location.

We settled on staying at my mom's sister's house that was an hour away from home—the home that was deemed unsafe. Angel, the family poodle, was boarded out to my mom's brother. My father decided to check at my uncle's house early on in our days of hiding in an attempt to find us. When he knocked at the door, Angel ran to the door like she normally did when someone came to the door, and my dad grabbed Angel and fled. Hours later, he called my mom and told her that he had Angel and if he did not hear back from her in a certain period of time, "the dog will be destroyed."

I remember hearing the tape later and the phrase "will be destroyed" stays with me.

Today, my mom says she did not realize she played the tape of my father's threat in front of us or in earshot. I remember my mom seeming to enjoy the drama of it all. She has always enjoyed the role of martyr. My father would now completely deny any such thing ever happened, or he would have some sort of spin where he was trying to protect us and was desperate. The dog wasn't destroyed by my father, and I can't recall how long we waited until it was safe to go home.

A few years later, the attorneys' concern actually happened. My father kidnapped me and took me to California. I was a great baseball fan, and one day he picked me up to take me to a baseball game. Only when I was in the car did he tell me that the game was in California. I remember being terribly excited about flying to California for a baseball game.

When we got to Los Angeles, he insisted on first driving me around to show me what a pretty place it was. Then the car broke down. He called the police for help and we went to a hotel. When he was in the bathroom, I called my mom to tell her I was in California. A short while later the police arrived and my dad was so impressed with their promptness to his call for help regarding the car. But they had come to arrest him because my mom had alerted the police that I had been kidnapped. I was briefly taken to a children's home, which I hated, before I was returned to my mom. As a result, I have always had a distrust of people who are supposed to protect you. Growing up, my parents were always telling me, "I need to protect you from your father," and "I need to protect you from your mother."

For years I did not hear from my dad—he just disappeared. Later I found out that apparently he had tried to contact us but my mother was always "shielding" us from him. She really didn't want us to have any contact with him. So we didn't. I'm the only one in the family who now talks to him, and it's not a lot.

Parents should try to minimize the stress on their children as much as possible. Making denigrating remarks about the other parent adds stress to children's lives. Similarly, purposely manipulating children and encouraging affection or attachment to only one parent is stressful for children and denies them the chance to have meaningful relationships with both parents. Children who are fed negative information about a parent and are asked to take sides in a dispute between parents may ultimately suffer from stress, anxiety, anger, and depression. These are children in despair.

In this case, a father conspires to keep his son from his mother and his siblings.

Eric is 42 years old and still carries the scars of his parents' divorce. He is the eldest boy and the second of five children. When he was 11, his parents divorced after a long and contentious battle. After the divorce, he lived with his mother, brothers, sisters, and maternal grandfather. His father remarried shortly after the divorce. All of the children continued to see and visit their father. When Eric was almost 13, he went on a fishing trip with his dad and never returned to his mother's home again. He did not meet his siblings again until he was 20 years old. His father created an elaborate, guilt-filled story about how he needed Eric to live with him and his new wife. He told Eric that, without him, he felt distraught and unfulfilled. He told Eric that his mother had the other children and so she no longer needed him, and, "besides, she never loved you." His father arranged for him to go to court to reverse the custody arrangement, and he insisted that Eric request that he be able to live with him and his new wife. Because of his desire to please his father, Eric told the judge what he had been tutored to say. Under the new court order, Eric was permitted to visit his mother and siblings weekly. His stepmother felt threatened by this new visitation arrangement. To appease her, the father was adamant that Eric return to court and request that the visitation be discontinued. Eric was to tell the judge that he no longer wanted to see his mother and siblings. Missing his mother and his family, Eric, throughout the years, attempted to contact his mother and his siblings by letter but never received any answers.

Guilty and sad about the choices he had made, Eric was fearful that, if anything happened to his father and stepmother, he would find himself homeless, because he had cut off all contact with his family and would have nowhere to go. It was a fear he lived with for years.

Thirteen-year-old Eric was used as the constant baby-sitter for his new stepsister and was exploited and treated cruelly by his stepmother. His father, who had a violent temper, never interceded on his son's behalf.

Eric developed into a fine young man. He was, however, always plagued by the feeling that he had abandoned his family and had been abandoned by them. As a result of these thoughts, he felt undeserving that any good should come to him and continually placed himself in positions to fail. Additionally, as an adult, he sought out relationships in which he could "save" people.

When he was in college, he attempted to contact his siblings and arranged a trip to see them in the city where they were now living. His father opened up Eric's credit card bill and saw the statement reflecting the charges for the trip. In a rage, his father threatened Eric that if he ever attempted to visit his family again, he would "strike him down from Heaven," even if he was dead.

At the age of 20, Eric found out that, for years, his family had attempted to contact him, even coming to the father's home in an effort to see him and leaving letters addressed to him. Eric, who felt that the family had written him off, was shocked and saddened that he was never told about or given the letters, yet was relieved to realize that his family had really wanted a relationship with him. It took many years for the family to build a bond with this young man. Finally, Eric was able to confide his fears of being homeless to his mother. His mother told him that he would always have her "and a home." Shortly after this conversation, his mother died suddenly. "When my Mom died, I lost her again. I felt parentless." He was, however, reassured that his mother had loved him, had missed him, and had spent years attempting to find him. He had never been abandoned.

The impact of parental alienation is pervasive and is not limited to children. This is a story from a father's point of view.

George and Mary grew up next door to each other. Their families attended the same church, socialized together, and the parents were in the same bridge club.

George and Mary married when they were in their mid-twenties. Although Mary had an affair with her professor during their engagement, by the time of the marriage, all seemed rosy.

The marriage appeared happy, and a few years later a little boy, Luke, was born. When the little boy was about three, Mary approached George with a dilemma. She had met another man and could not decide between the two men. She had written up pros and cons on both men and wanted to discuss the list with George. A divorce followed.

The divorce was amenable, and visitation was left unstructured. It was understood that George would have access to Luke whenever he wanted.

When Luke was five years old, Mary asked George for permission to take Luke to Hong Kong for six months to take advantage of a job opportunity. He agreed.

Unbeknownst to George, Mary was joining the "pro/con" man, Henry, in war-torn Cambodia. Hong Kong was a cover for the real destination. George would never have agreed to let his child go to Cambodia during a war had he known that it was the real destination. Eighteen months later, all Americans were airlifted out of the area, Luke and Mary among them. Upon their return to the United States, Mary married Henry, whom Luke referred to as Daddy. Luke never called George Daddy again. The child told George, his biological father, "the man who raises you is your daddy, and you're kind of like a friend." Eventually, Luke ceased to call his biological father by any name at all.

Luke was enrolled in a private school, and George paid half the tuition. He was, however, never invited to school conferences or included in school activities. After a few months, he approached the school and made an appointment to meet with Luke's teacher. The teacher showed him Luke's school papers, and he was astounded to see that Luke no longer used his real surname. The name on the papers was that of his stepfather. No amount of negotiations could restore the real name. It then became apparent that, in an attempt to erase George's paternity, Luke's mother had also changed Luke's passport and social security documents to her new husband's name. George feels that this was "identity theft."

Attempted visitation became a nightmare, and George sought legal action to ensure visitation. The strain on the child became apparent to George. Whenever he was with him, Luke was visibly upset, shaking, and overwrought. At one point, Luke blurted out, "You are taking Mom to court, you are trying to take Mom away from me." It was at this point that George dropped the lawsuit because he saw the "emotional wear and tear" on his child.

Over the next few years, visits between father and son were rare and strained. Despite George's attempts, there were no family holidays spent together, no vacations, no birthdays. George and Luke were kept apart. Mary accused George of being selfish if he wanted to spend time with Luke and distant if he tried to give Luke space. It was a no-win situation.

At a significant religious event in Luke's honor, George arrived early, and, as Luke's father, he expected to be seated in the front pew. As he was about to be seated, he was informed by his ex-wife that he could not sit there. An argument started, George demurred when he noticed his son's extreme discomfort, and he sat down in the second pew. Later, at the reception that George had paid for, Mary's cousin accosted him and said, "You are lucky you were even invited." His alienation from his child was made more explicit in his conversation with the clergyman, who said, "You're the father? You have never been mentioned."

It is only now that Luke (who is 42) and his father are beginning to attempt to reconstruct a relationship. George, upon reflection, concludes that there are lessons to be learned from his story.

> Insist on legal parameters and boundaries regarding schedules and visitation as a protection. Be firm about receiving respect. Always consider the child's well-being first. Be willing to temporarily let go with the hope that there will be a reconciliation at a later date. Be able to move on with your life and not be consumed with anger and bitterness. Acknowledge mistakes.

Not all cases of parental alienation are as straightforward. In this section, Frank, a youthful 71-year-old, recounts a childhood in which no mention was ever made of his absent father. Frank was 6 when his father left the family. His experience illustrates the damaging effects of parental alienation. The hurt can last a lifetime.

> I think I must have been about six years old when my father left. I was never told they were separating, let alone getting a divorce. I was used to my father being gone from the house because he was a soldier in World War II and was gone for long periods of time. He later was awarded a Purple Heart, and I have the medal. So he was simply "away." It was only later that I realized he was never coming back.
>
> I came from a working-class family on the West Coast. There were four kids. My oldest sister was 14 years older than my twin sister and I, and I have one other sister who is a year older than us. My oldest sister was married and out of the house by the time my dad left. I think she maintained a relationship with him over the years, but I'm not sure. After he left, we (my older sister, my twin, and myself) never saw him or heard from him for years and years.

Money was very tight in our household after he left—not that there was a lot beforehand. But after he left, things got very dire, and my mother went to work at a hospital as an aide. Those were the days before child support or the garnishing of wages, and she simply had to work to put food on the table. She was not educated. In fact, I don't think she even went to high school, and so she was forced to take a rather menial job. Later she took some courses and rose in the ranks and became in charge of all the nurses aides, sort of like a "chief aide"! At the beginning of her working, she would rage and complain about my father not providing money, but I didn't really understand it. I was, after all, only six. I did know, or rather quickly learned, never to mention him, never to ask about him, and never to ask any questions about finances. In retrospect, I know she must have been suffering herself. She was probably hurt, depressed, and anxious. I know the hours must have been long, the work hard, and then she had three kids under the age of eight waiting at home for her, and a "second job" to do. And, of course, divorce really elicits separation anxiety not only for the children but also for the adult.

I have one very powerful memory from those early days. My mother had taken us to visit her sister, who lived about an hour away. This was always a treat as my aunt, Pinky, who you'll hear about later, had no children of her own and so indulged us with cookies and things. As part of the excursion, we would always stop on the way home and get something cold to drink. California could be very hot in the summers, and in those days, with no air conditioning in the car, it was a welcome respite to pull into the gas station and get an icy Coke. Well on this occasion, my mother sent me in to get the cokes. She told me in a very firm, if not angry, voice not to spend more than five cents on the Coke "because since your father left, there's very little money." I went into the gas station and held out my hand with the coins in it and the clerk picked out the amount due. You see, I was still too young to be able to count money properly. As I was leaving with the beverages, the clerk said, "Tell your mother, soft-drinks are now seven cents." My mother was beside herself, she ranted, heaped abuse on my father, and, finally, close to tears herself, blurted out, "and he's never coming back." I'll never forget the shock and desolation I felt. Her words were a knife through me. I was reeling. And at the same time, I felt guilty that I had disappointed her and done something very wrong in wanting and buying the drinks.

Every child wants to please their mother, wants to make their mother happy, and I felt defeated. I felt that somehow I was responsible for causing her such anguish, that somehow I, too, had let her down. That scene is etched deeply in my memory—every detail of it—my hand with the coins, my mother's face, her voice, everything. Now that I think about it, that's probably when I was "told" that they were getting a divorce. I'm not sure that I processed the finality of it all. I may have chosen to think her words were said out of anger or rationalized it in another way. I, and most young children, can't really conceptualize such finality. It's incomprehensible. And I had no frame of reference. Remember it was the 1940s, and so I didn't know of any other family that did not have a mother and father. No one tried to explain anything to me or talk to me about it, and as time went on, I just came to accept it as part of my reality, my situation. Something awful but something that I could do nothing about.

As I just said, in the early 1940s, few couples divorced. So I never knew any other kids without a father at home. I only knew that our household was different and that there was a sort of shame about having no father around. It's interesting when I think about it, but my closest friend, later on in grammar school and all through high school, was a guy whose father had died. Interesting that I "chose" him as my closest friend. Not that we ever talked about our fathers or our grief. There must have been a silent sympathy in our shared fatherlessness.

A couple of years later I contracted polio and had to be hospitalized for over a year in an isolation hospital far from our family home. Since my mother was working and had two other young kids to take care of, she could only make the trip out to see me once a week. It was a horrible time for me. Frightening. Very frightening. I was in an iron lung and pretty sick. But as the months went by and I recovered, the kids in the ward became like a little family and there were even some good times. But my dad never came, never called, never wrote. Perhaps he was still fighting overseas, perhaps he was never told of my illness. I never asked and nothing was ever said. Maybe he did write, but out of hurt or anger or ignorance, my mother never delivered mail or messages. Sort of a kind of parental alienation where one parent sets it up so that the children are alienated from the other parent. It is probably one of the most painful and damaging things a parent can do to their child. Or maybe it's a fantasy that she alienated me from him, it's just wishful thinking on my part: maybe he just did not write or call. I'll never really know. Amazing that, at 71, much of this is still confusing to me.

I knew so little about my dad, and there was no one I could even ask. Since both my parents were originally from Texas, and since money was scarce, travel from California to Texas was not possible for us. I never ever even met any of my dad's family. I never met my paternal grandparents or my dad's sister, as they all remained in Texas. And after my dad left, the little contact that there may have been was severed. There were no birthday cards or Christmas gifts. I had no one I could talk to about my father and no avenue to find out about him or his whereabouts.

However, when I was 16 or 17, my aunt Pinky (my mother's sister) called me one afternoon and casually said, "Honey, come on over, there's someone I would like you to meet." My aunt Pinky had moved into our neighborhood, and it was not out of the ordinary for her to call and invite me to come over for some reason or other. So, unsuspecting, I jumped on my bike, and 10 minutes later was at her house. There was a man with her. My father. I can't remember what we talked about or if he even explained his abandonment of us. All I remember is that he smiled a lot and shook his head in amazement at my height given that he was a short man and I, at six feet tall, towered over him. From time to time, he would lean forward and touch me—my shoulder, my arm.

I don't really know why my aunt did it, why she facilitated the meeting. She and my mother were very close. It was both brave and disloyal on her part. Maybe she never told my mother and knew I certainly wouldn't, which of course I didn't! I can't even tell you how the meeting ended or what was said. Did he say he'd call, write? I don't know.

I do know that four years later, when my college sweetheart and I were planning our wedding, I was adamant that he could not be invited. Was that to protect my mother, or to protect me?

The only other time I saw him was when I was about 40. By then I had gained a PhD, gotten divorced, and had relocated to Chicago, where I was working and living. I don't know how he tracked me down, but he did. We drank a lot and talked of trivial matters. No questions, no answers. All I gleaned from our meeting was that he had been working as a ranger in Oregon and had a wife and a couple of kids. Perhaps they were her kids from another marriage?

He died about 15 years later. My oldest sister called and told me. I did fly back for the military memorial service and was given the U.S. flag that draped his coffin. It was very emotional for me. I have that flag, so perfectly folded in the way the military do. A flag but no father.

GOLDEN RULES

1. Children need both parents in their lives.
2. Don't give up being a part of your children's lives. Remember, children thrive with two parents. Even if you're not living with your children or are separated by distance, there are ways you can be involved and interested in your children's daily existence.

3. Do not use derogatory language or demean the other parent. Do not use insulting language or say insulting things about the other parent.
4. Consider your children's needs rather than being focused on "winning."
5. Allow your children their right to have a relationship with both parents.
6. Do not deprive your children of a parent no matter how you feel about the other parent. You will be harming your children.
7. Keep your own emotions separate and under control. Your anger, hurt, and dislike are for you to deal with. Don't impose these on your children.
8. Try and be supportive of your children's relationship with the noncustodial parent. It is for your children's good.
9. Do not manipulate or encourage your children to sever their relationship with the other parent.
10. Difficulties your children may encounter with the other parent can be worked through with a trained professional. Supporting alienation is not the answer.
11. Always think of what is best for the children.
12. Think of the future. Alienation from a parent will have long-term effects on your children.
13. Alienation from a parent can be supported only after speaking with a professional who recommends severing the relationship with the parent. Emotional abuse, physical abuse, sexual abuse, parental drug or alcohol addiction, or behaviors that endanger the children's safety are the major reasons for such drastic measures.

Six

Dos and Don'ts

> Most advice on child-rearing is sought in the hope that it will confirm our prior convictions. If the parent had wished to proceed in a certain way but was made insecure by opposing opinions of neighbors, friends, or relatives, then it gives him great comfort to find his ideas seconded by an expert.[1]
>
> —Bruno Bettelheim

Every year over one million parents divorce.[2] Divorce is devastating for the children involved. It is the death of a family. As difficult as divorce is, it can be made easier or more difficult by the behaviors of the divorcing parents.

DOS

Children's needs should be the priority. Often parents who are in embroiled in emotion-laden conflict impulsively allow their feelings to take precedence over their children's needs. When people are frustrated or angry, they can forget the consequence of doing this. This destructive behavior will cause great unhappiness for the children, who are left feeling helpless and fearful in this situation.

Do Take the Developmental Needs of the Child into Account. The age of the child requires different strategies. For example, in children under the age of two years, there often is an intense searching for the missing parent. Transitional objects, such as a favorite teddy bear or blanket, are soothing to the child. The child needs to understand that the parting parent has not disappeared or abandoned them. This is an age when children learn to trust. Parents should be aware that children may show signs of separation anxiety because they have been exposed to separation too early developmentally and have not mastered the idea of separation or object constancy (that if someone or something leaves, it is not gone forever).

Do Use Age-Appropriate Language and Details. Be aware of a child's developmental stage and cognitive and emotional abilities when explaining about a divorce. Younger children need simple, concrete explanations. Older children can deal with more complex explanations and detail. Children should not be told about the indiscretions, drug abuse, or homosexuality of the other parent. One must gauge whether it is something that should be revealed at a later time and whether it would be helpful to the child.

Do Allow Children to Talk Openly about Feelings. Try to keep any negative feelings you may have under check. Children should be free of the burden of dealing with their parents' emotions. Keep communications open. Be available for questions and make time to talk. Talk, talk, talk.

Do Remain Patient. Children may have to ask the same question over and over. "Will Daddy still live here after the divorce?" "Will you not be my mommy anymore?" "What is a divorce?" "Where will I live?" Sometimes children pose difficult questions, and it is okay to say, "I need to think about this for awhile" or "I don't know."

Parents Should Treat Each Other with Respect. Despite angry or negative feelings, politeness and civility are important, particularly in front of the children. Children need protection from further pain. Be considerate of the other parent's time with the child, and do not interfere with the agreed-upon schedule. Sudden schedule changes confuse children, upset the other parent, and cause friction. Any concerns or changes should be discussed between the parents without the children's presence or involvement.

It's important to be on time and dependable; never have a child left waiting on the doorstep. This is all too familiar a story. A child sits expectantly dressed and waiting for a parent to pick them up. Sometimes, a parent never arrives. This can be very traumatic for a child. Children should not be treated in a cavalier manner; parent's actions can haunt them forever.

The following recounts the experience of Chris, a 27-year-old man.

> I never saw him again. I must have been about 11 years old. That was the last time I saw him. There were so many times when he left me standing at the door waiting for him. I would be showered, dressed in fresh clean clothes with my hair all combed and slicked back. I would be so excited that I could tell him about my soccer or my new dog, and he would just not arrive. I would wait and wait and after about an hour I would just throw

> myself on my bed and lie there till my mom came home. He never even called to say he wasn't coming, he just didn't show.
>
> He did this so many times to me that eventually my mom decided that it was better that I did not get set up for such disappointment. She told him never to contact me again. And he didn't.

Be aware that parenting is a joint venture that lasts for the duration of your life and the life of your children.

Do Communicate Frequently. Both parents should be aware of what is happening in the children's lives, whether it is grades, friendships, or activities.

Do Keep Meaningful Relationships Undisturbed. Grandparents, uncles, aunts, and family friends provide constancy and stability for children when their world suddenly becomes unstable. Sometimes the extended family may feel it is a betrayal if civil relationships are continued. Sometimes the child feels it is disloyal to one of the parents if they continue the relationship with the extended family of the other parent. However, try to avoid disrupting previously important relationships.

Do Keep the Daily Living Schedule Intact. This helps to create a sense of stability for the child. If possible, stay in the same home. (Sometimes this is not feasible because of finances or job issues.)

Do Allow Children Time to Adjust to the New Living Situation. Children need time to adapt to a world that has turned upside down. During the adjustment, there may be regressions in behavior: bed-wetting, erratic toilet habits, a return to babylike speech and behaviors, volatile emotions, a drop in grades.

Reassure the Children That the Divorce Has Nothing to Do with Anything They Have Done, Said, or Thought. Children often feel guilty because they think they were the cause of the divorce. Reassure them that both parents love them even though it sometimes happens that both parents do not continue to be in the children's lives.

Do Present a United Front When Problems Arise. This united front sends a message to the children that both parents still care and are concerned about them, even if they are no longer married. This can be a double-edged sword, because children will sometimes create problems in an effort to get parents back together again.

Do Anticipate Difficult Situations. Important occasions such as birthdays or minor holidays such as Halloween or Valentine's Day (that are not spelled out in the divorce decree) can present potential difficulties for the children as well as the parents. It is important that children do not feel they are in a tug-of-war between parents. Try to be flexible, remembering to avoid unnecessary conflict for the children's sake.

Do Let Children Know That, Although You and Your Spouse Are Divorced, They Will Always Be Your Children and They Can Always Count on Your Protection. Miranda's parents divorced when she was quite young. Her father subsequently remarried a woman with whom Miranda has never been able to form any sort of positive relationship.

> I wonder constantly whether the experiences I have gone through with my dad have served any real purpose? It seems like sadness and anxiety and hurt have been the only constants in my relationship with him.
>
> I do know that I can never count on him. I do know that he will never be there to protect me. Like one time when he took me with him to visit his friend and let his friend's kids tease me and chase me around with a knife. Then, when I went to him screaming and crying he said, "Stop being a baby." Or when he lets his wife be nasty and mean to me and just ignores her behavior and does not put a stop to it. I do know that I feel he takes pleasure at seeing me unhappy. I do know that I can't count on him to return my phone calls. Sometimes, it takes him days to call back and then the reason I called doesn't matter any more. I do know that he does not know how to be a real parent.

The inability for Miranda to feel any sort of protection from her father has made her fearful that something might happen to her mother. "The idea of losing my mother depresses me." This fear has intensified her attachment to her mother and has exacerbated her separation fears.

Do Try to Keep the Marriage Together. In the words of Sulochana Konur, "As you stay married longer, you will find out things that are different about each other, not what is common about each other. And you have to grow together rather than looking for something in common."[3]

DON'TS

Do Not Present Catastrophic Scenarios. "Your mother will never see you again, she is running away from us all," or "We are going to have to move to a studio apartment, your father is not giving us any money." Avoid drama.

Do Not Use Condescending or Derogatory Terms When Referring to the Other Parent and Do Not Denigrate or Diminish the Other Parent. Children may identify with that parent and so feel denigrated themselves.

Do Not Use Inflammatory Language When Speaking to an Ex-Spouse in Front of the Children. It is painful, harmful, and confusing to children. Remember, children love both parents. These outbursts tear the child apart.

Do Not Play Games. Agreed-upon plans should not be broken or disrupted because of feelings of revenge or bitterness. The child is the one who really suffers.

Do Not Make the Child Feel Guilty. Respect children's love for both parents. Children should not be made to feel guilty over wanting to spend time with or enjoying spending time with the parent with whom they are not living.

> My mom would always give us the third degree when we—my brother, sister, and I—came back from visiting Dad. I always felt guilty that maybe we had a fun day and she was left alone, guilty that I had made the choice to visit him. She would make remarks like, "you know he is living in a very expensive part of town." She seemed resentful of any money or things he gave us. I love both of my parents but sometimes feel as if I'm not supposed to like or love my dad because my mother is still so bitter about the divorce.

Do Not Use the Children as a Weapon against the Other Parent.

Do Not Use the Children as a Tool to Manipulate the Other Parent.

Do Not Use Visitation as a Bludgeon against One Another. "This is not your weekend, I do not care if the circus is in town. I am not changing the schedule." Be flexible, the children are the priority.

Do Not Minimize Children's Pleasure or Enjoyment over Special Treats from the Other Parent. "Oh, she could spend money on a piece-of-junk toy for you but complains that she does not have enough money for groceries."

Do Not Use the Children as a Sounding Board for Your Own Problems and Concerns. Children should be allowed to be children. Talk to friends, parents, neighbors, ministers, counselors, and family members about your worries and concerns, not your children.

Do Not Use Children as Informants. Children should not have to spy and report back on what they see, hear, or observe in the other parent's home. Placing children in this position makes them feel guilty and disloyal and puts them in an untenable position. They feel they will anger the parent on whom they tattle and anger the parent who asks for the information if it is withheld. Questions such as, "Are you sure she doesn't have a boyfriend?" are to be avoided.

Do Not Have Disagreements or Arguments in Front of Children. Children should not be exposed to vitriol. Divorce is very upsetting, and they do not need further distress. Keep arguments private.

Do Not Ask Children to Keep a Secret. Telling and keeping secrets raises issues of loyalty, betrayal, and power. Avoid entangling children in conspiracies.

Do Not Put Children in the Middle. Do not make children choose between parents. They should be permitted to love both of their parents despite the parents no longer loving each other.

CAUGHT IN THE MIDDLE

Parents should not use their children as vehicles or weapons to continue their hostility and rage at one another. Children should never be placed in the middle between two warring parents.

The following letter is an example of how a child can get caught between two parents who continue to war years after their divorce. The child's resulting depression was severe enough to warrant hospitalization.

Dear James,

Miranda is in my room—heartbroken over your treatment of her. What I cannot understand is why you choose to treat her so poorly, to treat her with such cruelty. You might say you love her, but you do not. She has cried herself to sleep another night, and another night I sit and worry about how I am going to help her get well. All of this without any help from you. You could have prevented this: you could have treated her in a very loving and nurturing way. A caring and interested way. Instead you retreat, ignore, and are punitive. You don't care to understand her needs. I told her how punitive you are with me too. I told her she must get you to stop treating both of us this way.

Your issues with money are despicable. I've asked her to check if you are this cheap with your new wife and her kids. The lesson she has learned is about a father telling her to go ahead and get what she needs and it will be funded, only later to find out that her account is in fact unfunded. How many times have you done this to not only her but also to so many people, myself included. You are without heart. You are without feeling. You are unbelievable. When she came home today she told me that you make her nauseated and sick to her stomach. She told me that she can never feel relaxed with you and never has. She told me that you have always made her feel like a burden to you. How sad. I told her you always made me feel that way too.

Do not blame me for her expenses such as school books. Those expenses are your responsibility. You know that I have no money; otherwise, I would gladly pay for this. I told her this. I told her she has to get the money from you.

Sometimes parents use children to gain information about the other parent. "What's your mom up to? Is she still seeing Tom?" The child is put in the position of feeling disloyal to one of the parents if he reveals the information, disloyal to the questioning parent if he doesn't. No child should be asked to keep secrets, as Jimmy describes in the following letter.

Dear Dr. L.,

I don't know what to do. That's why I'm writing to you. As we left my dad's apartment, he said to me, "We are just going to stop and pick up Olivia." I asked my dad, "Who is Olivia?" He replied that she was a friend who was going to keep us company on the ride to camp. "Oh, and don't tell your mom. She'll have a fit."

We picked up Olivia, and I hated her. She had on tight jeans and she was all giggly. She sat next to Dad in the front seat, and I had to sit in the back. She spoke to me in this syrupy voice and I knew she was bad news. It really upsets me that I have to keep a secret from Mom.

I started feeling homesick even before I got to camp. I do not know what to do; do I have to keep the secret?

Will you write and tell me?

Dear Jimmy,

You need to tell your dad that children should not be asked to keep secrets from their mom or dad. It is too hard for a child. So tell your dad you cannot keep his secret. If there is something he doesn't want your mom to know about, he should not put you in the middle.

Talk to you soon,

Children can get caught in the middle of the parent's dynamics; they may see one parent as vulnerable, the other as stronger. In these cases, children may try to protect the more vulnerable, weaker parent. This was the experience described by a man reflecting on his parents' divorce.

I was always trying to protect my dad. I felt so sorry for him. He seemed so needy, so lost, so unhappy. Sometimes I would give up going to the movies with my friends, because I thought of my dad sitting alone. Sometimes I would even do things with him I did not like doing, like going to the grocery store. My mom somehow seemed stronger, more self-sufficient, less sad. I guess she was. She was the one who wanted the divorce.

Children can get caught between two divorcing or divorced parents when financial issues arise. "Ask your father to pay for it," or "I give your mother plenty of money, ask her." They also end up being messengers between parents with changes in schedules, vacation plans, or holiday arrangements. Parents should communicate to each other directly about such matters and not use children as go-betweens.

They were always warring about money. He would tell me to tell her that her child support would be late because his commission check had not yet come. She would send a message back: "Tell your father, 'Oh but you managed to buy yourself a new car without the commission check.' " I was always in the middle. One year I missed out on going to Disneyland. He told me

> to tell her that he would take me over spring break. I forgot to give her the message. By the time I remembered to tell her, it was too late for him to get the cheap airfare, so we didn't go. I never did get to go Disneyland.

The "forgetting" to deliver the message illustrates the child's conflicted feelings over money issues, separation, unfilled wishes of parents' reunification, regret over one of the parents being left, and guilt over being given a special treat.

The following is an interview with a 32-year-old woman who tells the story of being caught in the middle of her parents' divorce.

> I was only three and too young to remember any of this. But each of my parents when we were growing up would relate different facts about the divorce to us. Their entire divorce was open conversations at family parties, at dinners, on car rides, on the telephone. My mom had an opinion. My dad had an opinion, my paternal grandmother had an opinion, my maternal grandparents had opinions. It was always talked about. And everybody had mean things to say about each other. We were expected to take sides. My dad always wanted me and my older brother to side with him and talk some sense into my mother. We were sent with messages that we were supposed to relay to my mother or to my maternal grandparents. The effect on me was that I always worried about making everyone else happy; that was the beginning of my feeling that I had to make everyone happy around me. If I didn't deliver the messages, then they wouldn't be happy.
>
> Each week my father would give my mother a check—alimony or maintenance and child support. He would say, "I'm not giving the check to her until she does X, Y or Z," or "Give her the check and make sure she does . . ." And my mother, she didn't give direct messages. Her methodology was not direct at all, and hers was subtler. She would cry, and I'd ask, "Why are you crying?" "Because I'm alone," she'd answer. So I had this very aggressive dad and this weepy mother who was concerned and upset about money. If I went with my dad alone, I was the one chosen to carry the messages, otherwise my brother always did it.
>
> We tend to criticize our mother more. Our father has been less on the receiving end of our criticism. My dad was always trying to get us to come and live with him. Then Mom would say, "Your father should not be talking to you about those topics, he's such an idiot." And usually my grandparents would be over, so all my mother would have to do was deliver one or two lines, and then she would leave the room. Then my grandfather would go into a diatribe about my father. And then they would start to dissect him. This would go on and on.

When I was alone with my mother, she would be crying, and she wanted me to comfort her. And it was always about how she had wasted most of her twenties and thirties crying about him and it took her till she was in her forties to really start a new life again.

When I was the age of three to five, we lived with my grandparents. We went out to dinner, we went out to movies. My mom was never around, she would be working, maybe on dates. We never really knew where she was. I felt very cared for and safe when I was with my grandparents. I felt less of a financial burden when I was with them because they did not have the money problems that my mom had. Funny, at four and five, the memories from my childhood are fights about money, because that's what my parents fought about. My parents went to court all the time over money.

We never were brought to court, but our father would encourage us to talk sense into our mother. When things were really bad, his moods would show it. It was an enormous amount of responsibility for little children. I guess that's part of the reason why I've always felt I have to care for everyone but myself. I've always felt that I have to worry about other people's feelings, whether it's my mother or father, before I cared about myself.

I stopped going to see my dad when I was about seven. I would stay over at his house every third weekend. And then at seven or eight, I decided it was just too upsetting and I wouldn't go. There would be many incidents on Sunday night when it would be time for him to take us home, and he would play games with returning us to my mother. He was always passive, and he'd let his mother do the nasty stuff. There was never any control over our return. There was one incident where my paternal grandmother locked me in the bathroom at her house, so I couldn't return to my mom. There was a phone in the bathroom and I snuck a phone call telling my mom I was locked in the bathroom and they wouldn't let me out. I was pleading with her to come and get me. My mother didn't come to get my brother and me. My maternal uncle came and got us.

Years later, when my relationship got better with my father, I began to tell him about how we had been treated growing up. By the time I told my father how we had been treated, my mom had moved away. At that point I really learned I could depend on my dad. But growing up we were caught in the middle.

RESPECTING DIFFERENCES

A common issue in divorce is that the two parties have different philosophies of life. Different values and priorities may make living together impossible.

After divorce, going back and forth between two households that have different philosophies is difficult for children. Parents need to respect each other's differences and help children adjust to the differences. Religious differences, educational values, different household rules, and socioeconomic attitudes all represent different philosophical approaches to life. The following letter and response describe a woman's difficulty in handling her ex-husband's religious beliefs.

Dear Dr. L.,

Another dilemma, even though both Karr and I were raised in the Church, we have very different views as to how to raise a child. Karr insists on grace before meals, grace after meals, prayers at bedtime, and very specific behavior in Church. As you know, I am not an active participant in any religion. I don't mind Megan being taught about religion. I object to the fire and brimstone approach. She is being told that if she does not comply with Dad's beliefs, like saying her prayers or behaving in a certain way in Church, she will go to Hell. And now, she is fearful that she and I will not be together in an afterlife because I do not say grace at mealtime nor attend Church. What to do?

Grace

Hi Grace,

This is often an area that is problematic. Despite one's own feelings, one always has to keep the child's well-being as a priority. I think it is important to tell Megan that different people believe different things. There is a famous quote in *Hamlet*, "there is neither good nor bad but thinking makes it so." She needs to respect her father's views as well as your views. It is important that children learn and respect individual differences. Having said that, although Karr may believe that you will go to Hell, he needs to keep that to himself because he is traumatizing and upsetting his child. Perhaps you might want to forward my e-mail to him and invite him to talk this over with you. We know he loves his child and we know that he would not want to upset her.

Regards,

This issue can become more intense when different religions are involved: Christianity versus Judaism or Islamic thought, Hinduism, or Buddhist beliefs. All religions need to be respected. The basic principles of each religion need to be adhered to: kindness, respect, and decency to others.

For children, different rules in households are confusing and potentially problematic. Father is very organized, compulsively neat, and lives by rigid rules, whereas Mother is more free-spirited, and her household is not kept pristinely. Lack of consistency is confusing and promotes misunderstanding. The following letter illustrates what this is like for a child. As the response states, parents should attempt to negotiate these differences so the child is not caught in the middle.

Dear Dr. L.,

I am losing my mind. I am at my dad's for a week and already he has yelled at me 10 different times for not wiping the sink out with a towel or wiping the shower down after I have used it or messing up the fringe on the carpet. I guess you are not supposed to walk on the carpet or wash your face or take a shower. He always tells me that my mom is such a slob, and she has not raised me right. She did not raise me to be the perfect German solider. He expects me to take out the garbage IMMEDIATELY, he won't let me wait 15 minutes till my TV program is over. It makes no sense to me. Will the garbage multiply in those 15 minutes?

I am about to lose my cool, and we are in for a huge fight if this continues.

WRITE ME.

Colin

Hi Colin,

Yes, different rules are hard.

This cannot be new to you; you know your dad is a "neatnik." Perhaps it would not be a bad idea for you to talk to your dad and explain you understand that he likes things kept a certain way in his house, but he's making you miserable. Perhaps he could let up a little. He wants the visit to be a good one, and he may not realize this is putting a lot of pressure on you and making your visit difficult. You also need to tell your dad that he should not bad-mouth your mom. This is unacceptable and hurtful to you.

Parents often have different views on child-rearing practices. Some parents believe you finish everything on your plate, some value academic achievement, others value athletic prowess, some are more conservative, others are less rigid, some believe in working for extras while others are more financially indulgent. Parents should attempt to negotiate these differences so the child is not caught in the middle.

Regards,

The following interview illustrates how different philosophies affect raising a child:

> Tom and I came from different worlds. He grew up on a farm in the "fly over" part of the country, and I'm a New Yorker. I was given a lot—ballet lessons, piano lessons, ice skating, trips, summer camps. You name it! Tom has a very strong work ethic and believes children should work to have the extras. He thinks this is the only way a child learns the value of money. He believes I am lavish and indulgent with Rebecca and Max. He frowns on summer camps, fancy gym shoes, and travel abroad.
>
> Max is now a junior in high school, and we have a real problem. Tom thinks a state school with in-state tuition is just fine. Max is a bright boy and has a good shot at getting into Princeton, where my father went. Tom is adamant that no son of his is going to go to an "elitist" institution. Poor Max is in the middle. He really wants to go to Princeton, like his grandfather, and has many good memories of attending football games at Princeton with my dad. But, at the same time, he questions whether it is an elitist college and whether he belongs there. He so badly wants his father's approval and does not want his father to think he is soft.

GOLDEN RULES

1. The children's needs should be the priority at this difficult time in their life.
2. Don't use the children as weapons against your ex-spouse.
3. Don't use the children as "moles" who are expected to report information. Try not to press them for information about what happened when they were visiting with the other parent. Children usually feel uncomfortable offering information. If they do, listen closely and be supportive.
4. Don't make children choose between parents. Don't make them take sides. Children generally want to make both their parents happy.
5. Don't criticize the other parent in front of the children. Your ex-spouse is still your children's parent; when you criticize the other parent, your children may feel you are criticizing them indirectly.
6. Let your children be children, not your confidants.
7. Respect the other parent's values even if they don't replicate yours.
8. Be dependable. This offers comfort to children during a stressful time.
9. The age and developmental needs of children should be taken into account when helping them deal with this painful and upsetting event.
10. Patience, understanding, and empathy are vital.

11. Keep your own issues separate.
12. Be nonjudgmental with regard to the other parent.
13. Allow and encourage your children to enjoy their other parent.
14. Do not make children keep secrets from the other parent.
15. Do not ever put the children in the middle.

Seven

Grandparents, Uncles, and Aunts

A child needs a grandparent, anybody's grandparent,
to grow a little more securely into an unfamiliar world.

—Charles and Ann Morse

The following letter is from grandparents concerned about the welfare of their grandchildren.

Dear Doctors:

We heard you both on the radio and wanted to ask your advice.

We have a very difficult situation. We have two wonderful grandchildren that we saw on a regular basis and now we see only infrequently. The children loved coming to see us and we loved having them visit. They often stayed overnight and we would attend church on Sundays.

We do not consider ourselves extremely religious; however, we like to attend church on Sunday and say grace before meals. Since the divorce, our former daughter-in-law has become disapproving of us. She no longer wants the children subjected to our religious practices and so does not want us potentially influencing our grandchildren. We, on the other hand, feel it is important to give children religious values.

Our son has tried talking to his ex-wife about her depriving the children of seeing us. He has pointed out to her that a relationship with grandparents can be beneficial. She is adamant in not changing her position or her views on the children visiting us. Our son is reluctant to push the issue. We have tried talking to her, but she no longer takes our calls. We have even tried writing to her. I guess she feels that when she divorced our son she divorced us as well.

Dear Mr. and Mrs. S.,

This seems to be a difficult situation. It is important for children to have a continuing, loving relationship with grandparents. The support of extended family is important to youngsters, particularly after a divorce when children have already experienced upheaval and loss. The maintaining of relationships is important.

Since we do not know the family or your former daughter-in-law, we wonder if there are other underlying issues. Perhaps, your son could suggest to his former wife that a mediator or family therapist might be helpful in resolving this.

We hope, particularly for the sake of the children, that this difficult situation will be resolved.

Sincerely,

All 50 states have laws regarding the custody rights of grandparents. Grandparents petitioning for custody rights need to be aware that this is a complex process, and the help of an experienced legal professional is crucial. A strong case highlighting the reasons why the grandparent should be awarded custody is necessary. The best interest of the children is always the determining factor.

There are two basic rights with respect to grandparents and their grandchildren: custody and visitation. Custody is the legal right and obligation consistent with that of taking on full-time parenting and rearing of the children. There are times when parents are unable to care for their children, and the court may then award custody to the grandparents. This decision requires a major commitment on behalf of the grandparents.

Visitation is the other legal right grandparents are entitled to. If a family court judge awards visitation to the grandparents, the court sets a specific schedule of time that grandchildren are to spend with their grandparents. The applicable laws vary from state to state, so it is very important to understand exactly which of these laws do and do not apply to your own particular situation. If the court feels there is enough evidence to substantiate the fact that the parents are not acting in the best interests of the children, then the court will step in and act accordingly.

There are situations in which it may be appropriate for a grandparent to file for visitation rights. For example, when a divorce has become quite bitter and a custody battle has erupted, court-ordered visitation has been found to give the grandchild a sense of continuity and stability. This is especially true in the case where the grandparents are the parents of the noncustodial parent.

Sometimes the parents of the noncustodial parent realize that the parent's time with the child would be limited if they had to share time, and they do not wish to cut into that valuable, limited time. Under these circumstances, the grandparents may seek to obtain their own time with their grandchild. Other situations that often warrant the assistance of the court include those in which the noncustodial parent lives a considerable distance from the grandparent, making access to the grandchild less possible. There might also be a circumstance in which the grandparent does not enjoy a good relationship with the custodial parent, and visitation is rather limited or completely nonexistent.

Grandparents can be an important part of children's lives. They can be a source of support, nurturance, indulgence, permissiveness, warmth, and history. Children need stability and consistency. Following divorce, grandparents can play a particularly important role in continuing stability, and this relationship should be encouraged and valued.

One woman we interviewed recounts the positive influence her grandparents had on her life:

> My parents divorced when I was five. We never saw our father again. He just disappeared. But his parents, our grandparents, were wonderful to us even though we were living on another continent. They continued to call us, write us, and send us gifts. They were not going to abandon us like their son had. They are still a very important part of our lives.

It is important for grandparents to maintain a neutral façade in front of the grandchildren and not take sides in the divorce. A natural inclination is to take a son's or daughter's side against the spouse. Grandparents should guard against encouraging their grandchildren to take sides in their parents' divorce. It is in the best interest of the children that the grandparents maintain cordial relationships and be adaptable.

When in-laws do not get along well during a marriage, this can translate into problematic relationships after a divorce. The children, however, should not be deprived of an important bond with their grandparents because of angry, unresolved feelings. The animosity that was present in the marriage toward the in-laws is sometimes carried over when there has been a divorce, even when the court mandates that grandparents have visitation rights. The opposing parent may not comply with the court order, and, in such cases, there is little recourse.

In the following interview, Alexandra laments the loss of her grandparents after her parents' divorce.

> We did not see our paternal grandparents much. They disliked my free-spirited mother. After the divorce, they made their feelings obvious. They would indulge our cousins, the children of their daughter, with gifts in our presence, leaving us to watch and leave empty-handed. It was extremely painful and we felt dejected and rejected. Our maternal grandparents were quite the opposite. They were overly generous with us, often taking us on incredible trips abroad, paying for us to stay at grand hotels all over Europe. Their generosity and love certainly helped soothe the punishing attitude and behavior of our father's parents toward us. They punished us for the anger they felt toward my mother and the divorce.

In some situations the grandparents are more than willing to be involved, but one of the divorcing parents is resistant.

Dear Dr. L.,

It's me Kitty again. A new problem! Rick is making it really difficult for the kids to see my parents for Sunday tea. As you know, my parents are an important part of Janie and Sean's life. They were always going over to visit, doing fun things, and loved spending time with my parents. Now, whenever he gets wind of plans for them to visit my parents, he suddenly comes up with a reason to prevent the visit. The truth is he was really never fond of them anyway. We are fighting over so many other things that I do not want to add this to the list, but, at the same time, how can I let this go? The kids even say things like, "We miss tea with Nana and Granda." Rick just makes an excuse for why it is not possible. You have to understand tea was a very special occasion in that my mother put on an old-fashioned kind of tea, with fairy cakes, biscuits, scones, and usually a couple of kinds of delicious homemade cakes.

I would welcome any suggestions. I just don't know what to do. Any advice?

Kitty

Dear Kitty,

This often is a difficult situation because you do not want the children caught in the middle between Rick and your parents, nor subject to open displays of animosity between them. These displays are harmful to the children. As an aside, we hope that your parents do not say negative things about Rick, because this would only add fuel to the fire and put Janie and Sean in an untenable situation. Visits to grandparents should be fun and not fraught with negative tension.

You could remind Rick of the importance of a grandparent-child relationship and that you have encouraged a relationship with his parents. Or perhaps Rick's brother could mediate on your behalf so you do not have to get into it with Rick?

Regards,

Sometimes, in dire cases, there is a prolonged court battle between grandparents and a former son- or daughter-in-law over visitation rights. These are particularly difficult for the children, who are caught in the middle.

Mrs. G., an attractive and educated woman, was seen for a consultation.

My 41-year-old daughter divorced her husband five years ago. Initially, things were fine, and we saw the two boys all the time. However, three years ago, our daughter was diagnosed with cancer and died within the year. Since then, we have not seen the boys. Dan makes every excuse to avoid our seeing the children. Plans are made and cancelled at the last minute, he does not return our phone calls or e-mails, and we are beginning to feel desperate.

We have consulted a lawyer. The original court order stated that we were allowed visitation with the boys as long as it was a "minimal intrusion on the family relationship."

Dan has remarried and his new wife recently told us not to call again. I guess she sees us as an intrusion on their new family. Perhaps we represent a threat to her, being a reminder of our daughter.

We not only miss the boys but are anxious to know how they are doing. These children have been through a lot: first a divorce, then the death of their mother. And now another loss—us.

The role of grandparents in a divorce situation can be difficult. They must keep their judgments to themselves.

Dear Dr. L.,

I remember seeing you some years ago. We have now retired to Costa Rica and wonder if you could help me with my dilemma. As you know, my daughter was married with two children and has been divorced for two years. I never really liked Jesse because he was so principled about his socialistic philosophy. But he was a good father, and I didn't want to interfere in my daughter's marriage. However, when he lost his job and took to spending his days in coffee shops reading while my daughter was forced to support the family, I became increasingly angry at him. Later, it turned out he was having an affair with someone he met at the coffee shop. My rage knew no bounds.

My problem is this: the kids adore their father and are always talking about Daddy this and Daddy that, and it is very difficult for me not to inform them of Daddy's deeds. Do you have any suggestions? I know I should control myself.

I would appreciate any thoughts or suggestions.

Sincerely,
Caroline

Dear Caroline,

I guess Costa Rica is the new retirement place. I hear it is beautiful.

Understandably, as much as you would like to share your feelings about Jesse with your grandchildren, you do have to keep your feelings to yourself. Perhaps when they are adults, you can explain your anger at their father to them.

The children are already dealing with so much: the divorce, the upheaval of their family unit, and all the emotional difficulties associated with this situation. It is important that the children not have to mediate between their father and you.

Hope all is well with you,

Victoria and Tom approach everything in their life with zeal. They are passionately committed to family, and they can always be counted on for help and support. Now in their eighties, they still have the energy and verve that have always defined them. But they have experienced great pain and loss in their lives as well. Here is their story.

One of the toughest times to be a parent and a grandparent is to have to watch your daughter going through difficulties and to also witness your grandchildren confront the changes that are taking place in their lives, knowing that there is not much you can do to make it better. We thought that hiding our feelings helped and lent protection, but actually, in retrospect, it only confused everyone around. As a result of our silence, our daughter and grandchildren never knew how we felt.

Stanford was the first grandchild. Victoria and Tom were excited and thrilled to be grandparents and doted on their newborn grandson. Two years later, a granddaughter was born, and they were equally delighted.

A decade later, Sally, their daughter, and her husband, Mick, divorced. Shortly after the divorce, Mick married the woman he had left Sally for and moved to the East Coast. Sally and the two children remained in California.

Victoria remembers visiting her daughter and the grandchildren shortly after the divorce and being surprised and slightly taken aback at how 11-year-old Stanford had assumed grown-up responsibility almost overnight. She recalls Stanford explaining the morning routine to her, of which he was in charge. His mother had to leave the house in the morning before the children, and the boy had to be depended on to get himself and his sister ready for school and carpool pickup. He assumed the role of a surrogate parent. He had the morning routine broken down minute by minute. He had attempted to add an obsessive organization to his life so he could handle his deep unhappiness over his parents' divorce. His sister Miriam cried constantly, but Stanford, said Victoria, "constricted himself with a rigid structure, that was how he managed." Stanford carried out his duties with great seriousness, and both children were always ready on time. He revealed to his grandmother Victoria that he was unhappy over his parents' divorce, but it was better than all the fighting that had taken place between his parents.

Sally had decided to stay in Los Angeles before moving back to the Midwest so that Stanford could participate in the religious activities of becoming 13 with the children with whom he had grown up. She had scheduled the move back at the end of that summer, giving the children time to say good-bye to their friends and adjust to the idea of leaving their home.

Victoria recounted how the entire extended family had arrived in Los Angeles in June, two years later, to celebrate the coming-of-age festivities for Stanford. She remembers it being a fun-filled weekend packed with parties and visiting. And then Mick announced on the afternoon of the last party that he was packing up the two children for his summer visitation time and they were all flying out early the next morning to the East Coast. He was entitled to have the children over summer vacation. The children would never return to Los Angeles again, nor had they time to say good-bye to their friends and the families to whom they were attached. The next time they would see their mother was when she would greet them in a new state and in a new home. As grandparents, Victoria and Tom had no standing to prevent this abrupt departure.

At the end of the summer, the children arrived at their new home, and Stanford and his grandfather, who had always been close, began to form an even closer bond. They spent long hours together, talking, playing tennis, and being best buddies.

Stanford encountered social difficulties when he entered high school. Always a bright young man, he was placed in accelerated classes and endured teasing because of his academic abilities. Victoria and Tom began to notice that he became isolated, angry, and despondent. He engaged in furious exchanges with his mother and began to be unavailable to his grandfather. Victoria arranged with her daughter to seek help for her unhappy grandson. The therapist who was seeing the grandchild asked to meet with Sally and Victoria and told them Stanford was reluctant to tell them how he felt and so had asked his therapist to be his spokesperson: he wanted to live with his father as soon as possible. Sally refused the therapist's advice that her son should go live with his father immediately. Sally wanted to understand what was really going on.

Concurrent with these new behaviors, Mick had begun a custody suit in an attempt to take physical custody away from Sally. He instituted the custody battle upon his move east, and they were in and out of court constantly. Mick would spend long hours on the phone with his son, extolling the virtues of living in the east, apparently degrading Sally and blaming the grandparents (as being the deterrent to Stanford being allowed to live with Mick and the new wife). Mick would call, and Stanford "would be emboldened and all hell would break loose. Mick was fueling his anger. He knew how to influence him." Stanford's grades plummeted, and he began to fail all of his classes. In a hearing with the judge, he was told that he could not move until he brought up his grades.

Sally's home often felt like an armed camp, with Stanford berating her and constantly complaining about her parenting skills. He then would silently isolate himself in his room. The 15-year-old brought up his grades, heeding the judge's admonition. His mother attempted to persuade him to finish the semester at his present school, but his behavior was so provocative that Sally finally let him go. Stanford moved east, and Miriam stayed with her mother.

Victoria recalled that she immersed herself in work. "There was a lot I did not want to hear. I did not want to deal with the tragedy of losing my first-born grandchild." Despite the fact that they have close relationships with their other grandchildren, this could never compensate for the hurt that they experienced. "At 16, Stanford stopped speaking to us. For whatever reason, he was angry at us. He did not speak with us, nor did he speak with his mother. There were years of complete silence; it was as if we did not exist." Victoria and Tom continued to remember birthdays and special occasions with cards and gifts, but these overtures were met with silence.

Seven years ago, Victoria was diagnosed with a life-threatening illness, and Stanford flew in to see her. "It was a stilted conversation. I saw this little boy face on this tall body. It was shocking, he was all grown up. There was this chasm between us that could not be filled."

It had always been Victoria's feeling that once Stanford was old enough to move out of his father's house he "would come back to the family. I think he felt he owed it to his father to be loyal to him and not to others." Victoria finds it interesting that, when Stanford moved in with his father, he began to call himself Stan in an attempt to change his identity. Now when he speaks to his grandfather, he refers to himself as Stanford.

Victoria laments that Stanford did to his mother and sister what his father had done to all of them when he remarried and announced that "I got married and moved! No transitions allowed." He identified with the "strong personality." He bullied others just as his father had bullied him and cut off communication. He replicated his father's behavior, and, like his father, he was never held accountable for his deeds.

Although there has been a rapprochement, the blow of the broken years still lingers. The impact of the divorce has shaped Stanford's personality.

UNCLES AND AUNTS

Like grandparents, uncles and aunts often are affected by a divorce. They may have had a close relationship with a niece or nephew, and with a divorce that link is partially eroded. During the marriage, one of the partners may have played down their dislike of their spouse's siblings. After the divorce, they feel free to vent their true feelings. Visits and communication may be discouraged or even stopped by the disgruntled partner. The children may be encouraged to see their aunts and uncles in a less-than-favorable light. This is very painful for the children, because it is yet another loss at the very time that they need all the support that they can get.

With the loss of aunts and uncles, there also may be a loss of cousins, as seen in the following letter.

Dear Andrew,

I am glad your therapist has suggested you write. I, too, have missed seeing you and remember fondly all those wonderful summers we shared at the beach. So many memories.

Your letter caused me to think of what happened and how we lost touch with each other. I guess it all started about the time of my parents' divorce. My father was very angry and resented the support our mother's family gave to her. I remember my father saying disparaging remarks about most of mother's family, and the message to us was clear: "I don't want you maintaining a relationship with the Smiths." So much was going on at the time we really didn't think much about it. It was just another part of the divorce, and we accepted it. Somehow the years went by, and our lives went on. I guess we wanted to comfort our dad and please him and not cause him any more pain. So we did not protest or question. It was almost like his feelings became our feelings. You hear something enough times, you begin to believe it is so.

We did have so many good times. I would like us to try to build on those and get reacquainted.

Looking forward to hearing from you.

The situation illustrated in the above letter can be healed by making a concerted effort to maintain the connection between family members. This is the responsibility of both parents and the two families involved. Children of divorce should not be discouraged from pursuing relationships with their extended families. Grandparents, uncles, aunts, and cousins can offer additional nurturance and support.

GOLDEN RULES

1. No matter how you feel or felt about your former in-laws, remember that grandparents are an important support system for your children.
2. Do not disparage grandparents, uncles, and aunts.
3. Do not withhold visits with grandparents.
4. Permit continued relationships with grandparents.
5. Do not deprive children of grandparents who add richness to children's lives.
6. Do not inflict another loss on children by depriving them of their grandparents.
7. When a decision is made to divorce, decide how to tell friends and extended family, how much to say, and who should tell whom.
8. If you are the grandparent, try to remain in a cordial relationship with your former son- or daughter-in-law. This is in the best interest of your grandchildren.
9. If you are the grandparent, do not attempt to get your grandchildren to take sides or to influence them against the other parent.
10. If you are the grandparent, try to be flexible, and keep the children's best interests as your priority, which may mean initially seeing your grandchildren less often or for shorter visits. Be patient—it will lead to a better and more healthy outcome for the grandchildren.
11. If you are the grandparent, do not demean your former daughter- or son-in-law. This is a parent whom the child loves, and it will be hurtful and destructive to the child.

Eight

Changing Roles

> We can see that any happiness that we have in life is prone to change—it is the nature of things.
>
> —Buddhist lesson

With the dissolution of marriage, a new way of life begins. One is now a different kind of parent, and the family is now different. Parental relationships are changed, and there are shifts and modifications in responsibilities and expectations.

To help oneself and one's children, a new self-concept must develop: that of a divorced person. One has to put aside the anger, stress, and disappointment of an unsuccessful relationship and marriage and begin to work on becoming an effective single parent. Perhaps this is a role that was never sought, but nevertheless it is now the task that must be addressed.

It is normal to feel anxious and fearful when life is changing. It may feel as if the wounds from abandonment and disappointment will take a lifetime to overcome, but people can and do move beyond despair and hopelessness to a future of unanticipated possibility.

Divorced parents have to communicate with one another, have to come in contact and cooperate about children's and life's events: graduations, school activities, vacations, weddings, and special events. Divorced couples remain the children's parents forever. Research and clinical experience indicate that children fare better in a divorce situation when parents are able to get along and do not put their children in the middle.[1]

Ex-partners have to learn to be in control of themselves and their individual lives. There are pain, anger, disappointment, and resentment that have to be repaired in order to gain a much-desired equilibrium. Often one parent continues to feel anger and resentment toward the other parent and is unable to control his or her feelings. In these instances, the effects of divorce are seen on one of the parents, who continues to have a need to punish. Yitzhak Rabin, the late prime minister of Israel (1974–1977), noted, "You make peace with your enemies, not with your friends."

This illustrates the difficulty one father has in coming to terms with the divorce and custody situation. Their daughter is often hurt by her parents' difficulty with their changing roles. The girl went on a vacation with her father while school was still in session. The teacher sent school assignments for her to complete while on vacation so she would not fall behind. The homework was not done, and the child returned to school feeling overwhelmed, angry, and frustrated. The father resented his new role of having to supervise homework. When he was confronted with his lack of responsibility in not having the child complete her tasks, he lashed out at his ex-wife.

> Amy,
>
> You should really consult with me before putting your foot in your mouth.
>
> I have a note from her teacher saying that her homework did not come back from the copier and that she will need to do it when she returns. I was planning on having her do some extra work today when we returned until we were locked out of our house. That is why I dropped her off at 7:30 this morning. I know you feel that you need to sleep even though I am pretty sure you are not working for the next few days. I am sorry if you have to work three or four times a month. You have such a difficult work schedule.
>
> Laura had a great time, and I think that she does get an education outside of the school walls. She spent all of her time with a little friend and had to improve her sharing and socializing skills.
>
> D.

This is a father who has not come to terms with his changing role and thus resorts to repeated animosity and exasperation toward his ex-spouse in an effort to absolve himself of responsibility.

The separation of the parents in the process of a divorce is a difficult one for every member of the family. This is the time when the family starts to live in two different homes. Spouses are coming to terms with living separately as well as coming to terms with disappointment, frustration, and anger, and, although they no longer live together, they still have to negotiate their shared responsibility as parents. Both parents need to adjust to new roles and routines concerning the children. There is a great deal of stress stemming from loss and change. Each family member mourns the loss of the intact family. It is helpful if they work to create a "new normal" despite the old, unpleasant normal. Cooperation among parents living separately requires that both partners are able and willing to move on. This new definition of roles takes place in the context of other changing roles with extended family, friends, and acquaintances. Compounding all this are the difficulties created by the divorce process itself: legal considerations, financial disputes, custody and visitation decisions, and daily adjustment to a different lifestyle, all at a time when the children need time and attention.

FACTORS THAT AFFECT THE TRANSITION

The reasons for ending the marriage. The reason for why the marriage ended affects an individual's anger and resentment during and after divorce. If infidelity was the reason for the marriage ending, it leaves the abandoned person feeling a lack of self-confidence and bitterness.

Each partner's adjustment to the end of the marriage. Sometimes people have been married so long that their entire identity is tied to being a couple. In such cases, they may experience difficulty being alone.

The degree of animosity between the couple regarding legal and financial matters. The effect of the divorce can cause economic insecurity and embroil people in the labyrinth of the legal system. A person may be forced out of the marital home or may have to enter the workforce after many years, causing economic and emotional distress.

The decisions concerning the children. Custody and visitation difficulties can cause pain, frustration, and eruptions, or they can be handled in a smooth civil manner. Research indicates that interparental conflict that reaches high levels on a sustained basis has strongly adverse outcomes for children.

THE TRANSITION TO BEING A SINGLE MOTHER

Lilly, who had been a stay-at-home mother for many years raising three little girls, suddenly found herself needing to provide for the family after her husband deserted them. Despite a privileged upbringing that included a Swiss finishing school and a university education, she was forced to take a job as a clerk in a department store. Her world was upside down, and, because her shifts varied, there was no longer any regularity or predictability in her daily schedule. She no longer had the luxury of seeing her children off to school or being there when they came home. The effect on the children was disruptive and chaotic. Meals became haphazard, homework was unsupervised, beds were unmade, laundry went undone. The children had to take on responsibilities they never had before, and all of this occurred at the same time they were dealing with their father's abandonment. There was no immediate family to turn to.

Lilly's example is a dramatic illustration of the effect of divorce: the adjustment to the changing roles that divorce imposes on a family. No longer are there two people sharing the responsibility of the home, the finances, and the children. Seldom is there any preparation for the dramatic role changes. There is a change in identity and lifestyle. People are often overwhelmed, emotionally and physically. There is no period of adjustment before being thrown into a different role. Suddenly, decisions about finances, children's schedules, emergency contingencies, children's illnesses, and days off from school have to be made on one's own. There is no longer a backup partner to help shoulder the responsibilities and anxieties. Emotionally, all of this creates tremendous stress, anxiety, and upheaval for the parent and the family. Physically, it can be exhausting.

There is no preparation for being a parent alone. Suddenly, the custodial parent is responsible for everything: children, household functions, meals, and financial decisions. Socially, things might change as well. Divorced people may find themselves to be social pariahs. She is no longer part of a couple and is not invited to dinners, parties, or events.

THE TRANSITION TO BEING A NONCUSTODIAL FATHER

Rob had always been an involved father. Following his divorce, he had difficulty with the changes in his identity and his new role. He found it very difficult to adjust to not seeing his children daily and not being a hands-on father. Rob had always been the decision maker in the family, particularly regarding finances, budgets, and child rearing. His self-esteem was dramatically comprised. He was no longer in charge, and he became depressed. He did not know what to do with himself. His life had revolved around the family, and now he was alone. He had never developed friendships with other men or outside interests. His neediness became a burden to his children.

CHILDREN'S REACTIONS TO THE CHANGING ROLES

The parents of 13-year-old Jed were both schoolteachers. His mother had stopped teaching when he was born and was a stay-at-home mom. Both parents valued scholastic achievement. Jed's mother had always been very involved in his homework and school projects. After the divorce, the mother returned to work an hour's drive from the family home. She no longer had the time or energy to devote to buying supplies and supervising homework and assignments. Feeling alone and neglected, Jed's grades slowly began to drop, and he lost interest in his schoolwork. He was having difficulty adjusting to his parents' divorce and all the ramifications of the changing circumstances. There was a part of Jed that longed to be taken care of again and so he acted out by not doing schoolwork to get his parents' attention. His behavior was not a conscious manipulation but a cry for help: "Pay attention to me."

Parents should be alert to any changes in children's behavior following a divorce. When a change in conduct is observed, parents should take note: grades dropping, loss of interest in previous activities, different friends, a shift in standards, and other atypical behavior. These are all indications that the child is struggling and needs help coping with the new family situation.

Hi Dr. L.,

I'm going to make an appointment to see you real soon. You know with my new schedule and move, I have not been able to arrange the time for an appointment.

But I do have a question I need to ask you. I don't know what to do about Andy. As you know he is 15 and a sophomore in high school. Lately, I've noticed a few changes in him. Right after the divorce, he seemed fine. But now, eight months later, I am a little worried. He seems to be sleeping more, he does not want to go out with his friends, and seems to be content to just lie on the couch and watch TV. He's become a slob, and I have to fight with him to take a shower or even brush his teeth. At first, I thought this was just typical adolescent behavior, but, recently, his semester grades came out and they plummeted. He snaps at his father and me and always seems to be in a bad mood. I'm worried! What do you think?

Lynn

Dear Lynn,

What you are describing are the classic symptoms of depression: lack of energy, social isolation, irritability, loss of interest in previously enjoyed activities. All of this suggests he is reacting to the divorce. Is there a counselor at the school that perhaps you and your ex-husband could speak to? Andy needs someone to speak with about his feelings and the new family situation in which he finds himself. I would get Andy some help. Adolescence is difficult enough.

Regards,

Children attempting to adjust to their parents' divorce also have to adjust to the changing roles that divorce foists upon them. With their extra responsibilities, parents may no longer be as available as they once were for questions, help, and comfort. There is a great deal of difference between coming home with a latchkey and coming home to a parent greeting you at the door.

I remember coming home to an empty house for the first time. I wore the key to the house around my neck so I would not lose it. All day I clutched it. I felt really anxious that I might lose it and had to keep touching it to make sure it was there. I think the anxiety over the key was symbolic of the anxiety of losing my dad.

The key was to an apartment we had moved into. The house was gone, my dad was gone, the friendly, familiar neighbors were gone. I would enter and turn on all of the lights. I was sure that there was someone in the apartment waiting to pounce on me. The slightest noise would startle me. Before the divorce, my mom only worked part time and was always at home when I arrived from school. She would greet me at the door and give me a snack, supervise homework, and keep me company. Overnight too—it was a different world. I felt so alone and lonely.

The innocence of childhood is often lost after a divorce. Children sometimes become protectors of one or both of the parents. They may be placed in the role of confidant or holder of secrets (e.g., "don't tell your mother this," or "don't tell your father that"). Children may feel torn, disloyal, guilty, frustrated, and anxious. Too much responsibility and pseudo-maturity foisted abruptly on children is never healthy, no matter how old the child is.

Dear Dr. L.,

Our discussion in our last session made me realize how much my parents' divorce affected me. I am sitting on the tarmac again, once more delayed. I just wanted to tell you a memory I've had of my parents' divorce, so that you can remind me in terms of my own divorce and my kids.

After the divorce, my mom would encourage me to go out and throw the baseball with my brother. It was not the same as having my dad throw the baseball back and forth with me. I just lost interest. I began to hang out with the dope-smoking kids, cut classes, lost interest in school, and kind of gave up on everything. I probably would have ended up dropping out of school had it not been that my dad intervened and had me come and live with him. He insisted that I become involved in life again. No matter how late he came home from work, we spent time together, tossing the ball back and forth, watching TV, or just talking. He never put me in the middle or badmouthed my mom. Boy, I better remember that lesson. I remember reading in one of those news magazines on a plane that today fathers are more likely to remain close to their children after divorce than they were in 1971.

See you next week,

Jim

When a child's role changes from being a nurtured child to a protector of a parent, acting out may occur in an attempt to reestablish their former role and be taken care of. Rachel laments loudly and often that all she wants is to be taken care of. Her parents divorced when she was 14, and she was forced to emotionally take care of her needy, immature mother. At the time of the divorce, Rachel gained 70 pounds, which was her only way of nurturing herself. In an attempt to feel loved and taken care of, she became dangerously promiscuous. She spent hours on the Internet chatting with strangers and then meeting them in the park for sex. Rachel had tested into a gifted program, but after the divorce she dropped out of school. Her days were spent sleeping, ordering pizza, making popcorn, watching television, and scouring the Internet for men (in an attempt to get attention). It was only after she developed a sexually transmitted disease that the gynecologist insisted on referring her for counseling.

GOLDEN RULES

1. Be aware that the changes in roles are difficult for everyone in the family. Time to adjust is needed.
2. A change in roles and status should not demean self-worth.
3. Be aware that there are many new roles that will have to be learned such as disciplining, communicating, housekeeping, and financial responsibility.
4. Understand that everyone's role in the family has changed.
5. Each partner is now a head of household and needs to assert his or her authority. Children have to adjust to this change.
6. As decision-making roles change, don't discount your children's point of view.
7. Be upfront with your ex-spouse about changes that the new roles have necessitated.

8. Accept advice regarding negotiating a change in role. Listen and try not to be defensive. But also be discerning about the advice given.
9. Changing roles is a time of learning. One is not expected to know all the answers.
10. Try not to be overwhelmed with all the changes. A little humor helps.

Nine

New Relationships

I dwell in Possibilities—
A fairer House than Prose.

—Emily Dickinson

It is not uncommon for children of a divorce to carry the fantasy of being able to reunite the parents. This can be a conscious or unconscious wish. Despite the terrible fighting that sometimes occurs and the relief that the divorce brings, there still may be a wish to reunite the parents. Children harbor the wish to have an intact family and be "like everybody else." All of this makes the introduction of a parent's new relationship problematic. It is a situation that should be handled delicately.

The timing of an introduction has to be well thought out. Children need an opportunity to digest the divorce before dealing with the introduction of a new person. Separation on Monday, introduction on Saturday is not a good idea. The children should be introduced to a new person in the parent's life only after a new relationship has become firmly established and there is a serious commitment. Children should not be introduced to every casual relationship. There is no reason to further upset or involve the family. Timing of introductions must be very carefully thought out. In the following letter and response, Jim, smitten with Carole, impulsively and somewhat naively wants to immediately recreate a happy family.

Hi,

I am sitting on the tarmac and thought I would use the time to ask you a few questions. I told Joanne I wanted out. She immediately brought up

Carole. Remember she saw us at the restaurant, and later I fessed up. My questions are: Do I tell the children about Carole? When can I introduce the children to Carole? I know the kids will just love her. She is such fun and so young and peppy, loves children, and cannot wait to meet mine. Can I bring her to the spring carnival at school? I think that is neutral territory, even though I know Joanne will have a fit.

Best,

Jim

Jim,

I know you have been unhappy for a long time. Since you have only known Carole three weeks, I think it is a little premature to tell the children. Why don't you wait until the relationship is more established before you introduce her? Perhaps after a few months you might consider the introduction. After all, it is not a wise idea to put the children through multi introductions of new women in your life. You do not want to introduce them to every Tess, Bess, and Carole! Only if you are involved in a serious relationship should the children meet the person.

As much as you are taken with Carole, I doubt that the children will be as enthusiastic as you are. You must remember that they will still be reeling from the recent separation and breakdown of the family unit. They need time to digest what has happened, to process the changes in their lives, and to understand the impact of what divorce means. I think at this point they will have very strong feelings and reactions to their mother being replaced. For these reasons, it would be far too premature to bring her to the carnival or anything else. Should the relationship with Carole mature into a permanent one, the children will always see her as the reason you left them. No matter how special a person she is in your view, the children's feelings toward her would always be tainted should the introduction be made prematurely. The timing of the introduction is therefore critical. Don't act rashly.

Regards,

Introductions need to be gradual. Children need time to get used to the idea of a new person as well as to the new person. The children need preparation before the meeting. Incremental exposure is helpful. An intense weekend of togetherness with a stranger is likely to be difficult for children.

In Jim's next letter, he is even more anxious to introduce his children to Carole. But it is still too early.

Hi Dr. L.,

Carole and I have been together since Christmas, that's six months! I remember what you told me about acting precipitously. Can I introduce her to the children NOW?! On my next weekend with the kids I thought I would plan a couple of days at the lake. The children could swim, we could all picnic, and there is a water park nearby. We could have a campfire at night, tell ghost stories, and roast marshmallows. (Carole can really weave a tale!)

It would be such fun for the kids, and Carole cannot wait to meet them all. Is my plan naïve or acceptable?

Best,

Jim

Jim,

Your idea is wonderful. But not yet. Carole needs to be introduced gradually to the children. The first meeting needs to be short and sweet. Perhaps, all go out for an ice cream together or go to the playground or go out for hot dogs. Make the first meeting short, casual, and not too intense.

You need to prepare the children before they meet Carole. In a relaxed, informal way, tell the children that you have a friend that you would like them to meet. Tell them her name is Carole and that you like her and that you hope that they will like her too. They might ask you if she is your girlfriend. In which case, you'll say yes. They may ask, "Does Mom know?" and you'll say, "I don't think so." They then may say, "Can I tell Mom?" You need to agree, because children should not be asked to keep secrets that will put them in the middle. Maybe, out of anxiety or curiosity, they'll ask if you are going to marry her. I suppose the best way to answer this is to tell them that the decision has not been made. This may lead to more questions such as, "If you marry her, will you have more kids?" If confronted by unanticipated and difficult questions, you can always say, "Let me think more about that question." But do get back to them with the answer. This is about trust, and your children need to know they can trust you.

Explain to the children that they do not have to love Carole or even like her, although you hope they do. But remind them that they have to be courteous and polite. Just like you may not like their friend Mary Jane as much as you like their other friend, Victoria, they may not necessarily like Carole. Remind them that neither Carole nor anyone else will take the place of their mother. They have a mother; nothing can change that.

Regards,

When children are present, behave in an adult, mature, and appropriate manner: no giggling with delight at each other, no "kissy face," no chasing each other around the house, no gazing longingly into each other's eyes, no stroking each other. There is plenty of time for physical affection when the children are not present. Children are still reeling from the divorce and dashed hopes of the reunification of their parents. They need time to accept that their biological parents will not be reunited. It is only after they are more familiar with the situation and with the new person that modest affection should be shown. Start and end with hand-holding.

To help children adjust and diminish competition, share yourself equally between the person and the children. For example, when you go the movies, place yourself in the middle so the children are one side and the new person is on the other.

Rose, a 15-year-old, is having difficulty adjusting to her father's status as a single, dating adult.

> I sort of blame my dad for my hatred of Kimmie. He was always touching her, whispering things in her ear, and playing with her hair. The first time I met her, they were all over each other. I wanted to hit him. I thought of my mom with no social life, just always working and taking care of us. I just wanted to hit him. Dad and Kimmie looked like the kids you see in the mall. It was revolting.

SLEEPOVERS

"No sleepovers."

"You're kidding!"

"No sleepovers."

A parent who is in a new relationship needs to be sensitive and mindful of children's emotions and feelings. Children dealing with the tumultuous feelings surrounding divorce should not have to deal with their parent's sexuality. It is not necessary. Children accept that married people sleep in the same room and in the same bed. Children accept the social convention of long-term committed couples sleeping in the same room.

Josh's letter below illustrates how a 14-year-old boy reacts to his mom's boyfriend sleeping over.

> Dear Dr. L.,
>
> I am glad to be out of Mother's house, it's my week at my dad's. She introduced us to Gregg on Monday, and on Friday he stayed over, and Saturday morning there he was. Yuck! There are some things I don't need to know,

and don't want to know. It is really upsetting. I tried saying something to her, like you suggested. She just laughed and blew me off. Can I ask her to come with me to my next session? Maybe you can get through to her.

Dear Josh,

I am sure it is very upsetting to see your mom in an intimate relationship and have your mom ignore and laugh at your reaction. Bring her to your next session and we will all talk about it.

The following letter was written by a 15-year-old girl whose parents were divorced when she was 13. It was brought to a therapy session.

Dear Dad,

I am writing to you because I do not want to have a long drawn out "talk" with you. I do not care what you do with Kimmie, but don't ever have her sleep over at the house with you when I am there!

Rose

It is not always easy being sensitive only to children's needs. Sometimes the parent is caught between the child and the new partner. Phyllis, a 46-year-old, reported her chagrin at being told by her recently divorced boyfriend that she would have to sleep in the guest room because "I am not going to do that to my 13-year-old boy." Her fury increased the next morning when her beloved carefully set the breakfast table for his son, made pancakes, and set out yogurt and fruit for him while she was offered only a cup of coffee. "I couldn't believe it. Why was he doing all that for a 13-year-old and yet doing nothing for me?"

Sometimes both halves of a new couple have children. This can be a difficult situation, particularly when the children display jealous and competitive feelings toward each other or when the children do not like the other children. When one part of the couple dislikes the other person's child (as described in the following quote), professional help may be necessary.

I really like her, but I can't stand her 10-year-old son. He's spoiled, obnoxious, and bad mannered. I can't imagine living with him. I don't want to hurt her feelings by talking to her about it, but I have to wonder if there is any future for this relationship.

Today people often choose to live together rather than commit to the legality of a marriage. Frequently, divorced people, now a little "gun shy," opt to live together. This, of course, necessitates sensitivity to the children's needs. This arrangement cannot be done precipitously and requires planning and delicacy.

The new person needs to meet the children, form a relationship with them, and give them a chance to adjust to the living arrangement. Time and patience are critical. The children's needs must be considered carefully, and they cannot be dealt with in a cavalier fashion. Moving someone in with little prior thought or planning can have negative ramifications.

In the following quote, a woman recalls her mom's boyfriend moving in.

> I remember coming home from summer camp. I knew about Dave. Mom had sent me a letter asking, "How would you feel if Dave moved in?" I was 12 years old; what could I say? I knew she would have him move in regardless, so I did not reply to her question. I didn't expect him to be fully moved in when I came home from camp—that was a shock. Then it got worse. The very first night we were going to celebrate my homecoming at my favorite Chinese restaurant. But Dave had other plans; he had his favorite Chinese restaurant. We got into a terrible fight. Imagine fighting with a 12-year-old? The worst part was that my mother supported him. It was all too much: missing my dad, missing the intact family, the divorce, trying to adjust to the divorce situation, and then Dave. My mother seemed oblivious to all of it.

The next letter and response describe a boy's feelings about his mom's boyfriends and her lack of sensitivity to his needs.

> Dear Dr. L.,
>
> I arrived at my grandma's yesterday, boy am I glad I'm here. Everything is the same. It's so great. Nothing has changed since the last time I was here. My room is exactly the same as I left it—same comforter—the radio is right next to my bed, like it always was. Even my red cup for water is still on the bedside table. It all gives me a feeling of being safe.
>
> The day before I left for the summer, my mother moved Fred in. Dr. L., do you realize this is the third guy she has had living with us? Boy, am I glad to be out of there. She never gives me time to even get to know them, and wham they're in. Just as I'm getting used to them, and maybe even like them, they're out. They are fighting, she is crying and saying, "I can't do this anymore," and I'm just stuck in the middle not knowing what to do. She never thinks of me. Why can't it just be the two of us? Boy, am I glad to be at my grandma's.
>
> Brad

> Hi Brad,
>
> Yes, it is very difficult to have people move in and out of your life with little preparation. How would you feel if I asked your mom to come and talk

with me while you are at your grandmother's? This is what I would talk to her about. I would explain that:

- Children need to get to know someone before they move into the family home.
- Parents should allow themselves plenty of time to know that a relationship is very serious and will probably last before even considering a live-in situation.
- It is very difficult for children to have one person after another move into their home, let alone have one person move in and out.
- Having people move in and out makes children put up a barrier, and they learn not to become attached to people.
- Time should be taken to talk to the children about someone new moving in.
- Children need time to absorb the news and digest it. After presenting the news, there should be a waiting period that gives the children time to ask questions and make their feelings known.
- Parents should not expect the children to be delighted.
- Children may feel that they are being disloyal to the other parent.
- Children may feel resentful or displaced in having to share the custodial parent.
- It is not wise to ask the children's opinion or advice on how they would feel about someone moving in.
- Perhaps your mom could give you some advance warning in the future. She may say something like, "Bill and I have become very fond of one another, and he is going to be moving in with us in about a month."

Hope this helps.

Regards,

INTRODUCTION OF TWO FAMILIES

Frequently, a divorced parent will meet someone who also has children. Bringing two families together can be challenging. There are now not only the children and another adult competing for the parent's time and affection, but the children must also now adapt to the new person's offspring. Jealousy, competition, dislike, and anger are some of the potential issues. It is imperative that parents talk and listen to the children at length, before introductions. Time needs to be set aside to talk with the children about their feelings throughout the process of blending. The following letter and response provide an example of some common issues that arise in blended families.

Dear Dr. L.,

I cannot believe three years have passed since we last spoke. In that time I got divorced and got joint custody and met Lisa. She is fabulous! I do not think she is a narcissist! She has two adorable little girls, ages three and five, and was a second-grade teacher.

But here's the problem: my kids don't particularly like her and really dislike her children. They say they are bratty and demanding. They hate my involvement with Lisa's kids and stomp out of the house when she's over with them.

Kate, who is now 16 (can you believe it?), has threatened that she will not live under the same roof as them and will live with her mother full time if we move in together. I fear that Frank will do the same thing. I don't want to lose my kids; I don't want to lose Lisa and I DO want to move in with her. I am tired of being alone. The little girls really are adorable. Do you think it is jealousy and that with time they will get used to the girls and Lisa?

Would you mind answering these couple of questions? Other than this small problem, life is great.

Hank

Hank,

Nice to hear from you again. This is not a small problem. Nor is it an uncomplicated one. I think you need to talk at length with your kids and find out why they do not like Lisa. Have they known her long? Did they like her initially? Did their feelings toward her change?

This is a delicate issue. Are Frank and Kate feeling displaced by the introduction of other children? Are they jealous of your attention to and affection for the little girls? Kate's threat of moving out is serious. Clearly, she is not happy or comfortable with the new situation. It may be manipulative, a cry for more attention, or an attempt to gain power. She became the woman of the house when you and Freda divorced. Does she feel her role has been usurped? You need to spend a lot of time talking to her. Talk quietly, privately, and in a relaxed setting. She may end up living full time with her mother. That certainly is a possibility. You need to think about the consequences of blending the families. There are always consequences to actions. This is about balancing everybody's feelings.

Regards,

In the following, a young woman reflects on the true challenges of her mother's remarriage and the blending of the two families.

> We were like two camps. His kids versus us. I think it was her second marriage. We hated each other. I was eight and they were teenagers. They picked on me all of the time. They must have known their father left their mother for my mother. I was always running to my mother crying and she would yell at them. I was glad when they eventually got divorced. I guess the combining of the two families was a tremendous strain on the marriage.

When families are blended, it is important that only the biological parent discipline his or her children. Resentment and anger are exacerbated when a stepparent disciplines stepchildren. This, in turn, ultimately can lead to problems for the couple.

Miranda reflects on how the animosity she showed toward her father's new wife may have contributed to their divorce.

> He remarried when I was about 12, a witch of a woman. She was ugly too. She once chased me around the house trying to cut off my long, black, glossy hair. She said it was ugly, something I believed for years. Now, of course I realize she was jealous of me. She had a child of her own, a boy called Scott, who was a few years older than me. I remember feeling very jealous of him and sad because my dad would give him money for stuff like golf lessons and he couldn't even pay child support for us. I was glad when they got divorced. But then I felt a little guilty for the part us kids probably played in that divorce.

When parents remarry, there are sometimes difficulties between the ex-spouse and the current spouse. Competition, different values and philosophies, and financial concerns can create conflict between the adults. To diminish the conflict, it may be wise for all of the adults to meet and acknowledge their roles and show respect for one another. If this cannot be accomplished in a mature manner, a professional's presence may be necessary to keep the meeting orderly and on track. For example, the man may say something like, "You were my first wife, you will always be my first wife. You are the mother of my children. You will always be the mother of my children, and that will never change." He may then turn to his new wife and say, "You are my second wife and I love you. My life is now with you." In this way, respect is afforded to both women, and acknowledgment of the reality prevents either party being threatened.

Sometimes it is difficult for the person in the new relationship to fully understand the children's emotions. Take, for example, Steve's letter to his therapist about his new current girlfriend, Cathy.

Dr. L.,

I was reading several e-mails from my sons this morning, and I am pretty sure the letdown I felt last evening had to do with the loss of the long-term relationship with Anne (the first wife) that impacted me at the end of the day. It is only now that I fully realize that Anne is not going to change, that our relationship is not going to improve, and that I could not live in the small world that Anne has settled into.

I think subconsciously it kind of got to me. A sense of loss happened at the end of a great day with my family—a family that will never be the same because the parents have gone their separate ways. Our family dynamics are changing. This will probably be the last year that it will be just Anne and I with the boys at Thanksgiving and Christmas.

Thankfully, Cathy was there for me later last night. It was hard putting my feelings into words last night. I had almost shut down and could not articulate what I can today. I know she must have been perplexed at how aloof I must have seemed. I think I became more and more quiet as the evening wore on. I kept thinking how sad it all was for the boys as this would be the last holiday with both of their parents.

Thanks,
Steve

Sometimes when an ex-spouse learns that the former partner is involved in a new relationship, he or she seeks solace through destructive habits and manipulations. Such is the case in the following e-mail exchange between Steve and his son Charlie.

Dad,

I really care for Mom and feel for her when she is having difficulty, but I do not plan to reach out any more than I have already. This is part of the game she plays that we have discussed in therapy. She closes off as a way of control. I have no desire to play. It is hard for all of us. I just try and keep in perspective the difference between the mom that I knew and who appears every once in a while and the person ravaged by alcoholism and drug addiction resulting in the nonsensical rationalization of her own life and actions.

It is sad, but we cannot change it.

Charlie

Dear Charlie,

Thanks for reminding me of the futility of dealing with someone who doesn't want to get better as much as we want her to get better.

Dad

Sometimes it is difficult for the person in the new relationship to fully understand the mixed emotions of the children. Sophia consulted with her therapist before meeting her boyfriend's children. She was careful to give the children plenty of attention and to temper her feelings toward their father. The children loved her, and she was then invited to one of the children's birthday celebration, which was to take place over the weekend. She arrived with special homemade cookies. The nine-year-old, somewhat surprisingly, given how well the dinner had gone, said, "I hate these cookies." Later she opened the birthday gift that Sophia had brought and declared, "I already have this dress, my mother bought it for me."

Youngsters attempt to cope with the trauma and confusion of divorce to the best of their abilities. Many times, not having the words or the experience to explain their feelings and thoughts, they express their emotions by their behaviors. A parent is hurt and confused when children scream, "I hate you" or erupt into a tantrum. "What am I doing wrong?" is the plaintive question heard from mothers and fathers. At these times, it is important to remember that children are simply displaying how overwhelmed they are by the divorce and its consequences.

Laura's parents divorced when she was just a baby, and six years later they remain in constant and continual conflict. Six-year-old Laura was referred because she had seemingly lost her cheerful, good-natured personality. She now has frequent temper tantrums, cries much more than she had previously, and alternately clings to her mother and then erupts into angry outbursts. Laura's mother remarried after she was divorced from Laura's father and recently divorced her second husband.

Dear Dr. L.,

I am attaching a note from Laura's teacher I received today. I feel I try to do everything humanly possible to create a safe, stable environment for her. What am I doing wrong? What can I change?

Amy

Teacher's Letter

It is upsetting to me that I have to write you this e-mail because Laura had such a fantastic day at school yesterday.

Today she and another child were taking a long time to come back from the bathroom. When I went in to check on them, she had the child pinned up against the wall and was saying, "I told you not to flush the toilet, it will overflow." Laura and I had a conversation about this and how her actions were bullying. She had a time-out during recess, and she said she was sorry to the child. I told her I was going to talk to you about her behavior. I also explained that this was unacceptable behavior in my classroom.

She was also having a difficult time concerning her birthday party. She told a classmate that she couldn't come to her party. Later when the same classmate said, "I don't want to come your party," she got really upset and said she might as well cancel because no one was going to come. I tried explaining to her the consequences of what she said earlier and why that child said she didn't want to come. I am not sure she made the connection.

Please have a talk with her and let me know if there is anything else I can do to help Laura along. Have you given any more thought to signing the permission paper I sent home, so that I can speak with her counselor?

Dear Amy,

Laura is angry with both you and her dad for the divorce. (People only dare to show their vulnerabilities to those with whom they feel safe, trust, and know that love will not be withdrawn.) And so you are the recipient of all her rage. She feels truly safe with you. Her father's announcement of his plans to remarry has thrown all of her thoughts of family reunification into turmoil.

Apparently, Laura feels that if she is perfect and meets all of your expectations (good grades, paying attention, and good behavior at school), she will get what she wants—the three of you living together, no more court battles, and a loving intact family. When faced with the reality of her fantasy breaking apart, she falls apart. Her conduct with her little classmate is very upsetting and unacceptable. Having said this, I think this is the explanation. She is displaying what she feels happens when someone does not follow instructions and rules, "I told you not to flush the toilet, it will overflow." Perhaps she was fearful that both her teacher and you would blame her for the mess in the bathroom and that the two of you would be angry and disappointed in her. In her mind, by losing control of the situation in the bathroom with her classmate, she now feels she is not totally in control of everything. Without this magical total control, she cannot control her father's rejoining the family. In this way, she feels responsible for her father's impending engagement. She feels "bad" and imperfect. When she exploded into tears over the possibility of no one coming to her birthday party, she exhibits how she feels about herself: "No one loves me or cares about me."

This explanation only attempts to clarify Laura's behavior. It does not tell you how to make it stop. Talk with her about how she is feeling. Tell her again and again that she is not responsible for the divorce. Tell her over and over that you love her. Tell her that, as much as she wishes and hopes that you and her dad will remarry, this is not going to happen even if you both remain single. Tell her that she does not have to attempt to be perfect. Tell her everyone gets upset or angry, even grownups.

Hope this helps a bit.

Laura's symptoms are a disguise for her fear of abandonment. She felt rivalry toward her stepfather and experienced betrayal when her mother remarried. She was then elated, guilty, and fearful about her "victory" and felt empowered when the stepfather left the marriage. Would she too be cast out and never see her mother again? Additionally, Laura's behavior suggests that she is having trouble with her father's upcoming marriage and reveals her fears of abandonment and anger concerning the marriage.

Parents' needs and children's needs and emotional well-being are different. Children may not be ready to embrace a parent's new relationship. Therefore, it is essential that the parent be patient and sensitive to the children.

GOLDEN RULES

1. Do not introduce every new boyfriend or girlfriend to the children. Only introduce people when the relationship is serious.
2. Talk to children about a new relationship ahead of time.
3. Avoid competition. If you are the ex-spouse, keep in mind that it is helpful for your children to have one more encouraging, loving adult in their life. Try to avoid thinking of them as the new spouse, and regard them as someone who is potentially important to your children.

   If you are the stepmother, let the children's mother know that you do not want to replace her, you want to help take care of the children. Ask her for schedules and special accommodations that the children might require.

4. Do not automatically regard the new partner as an adversary. Do not assume that the stepparent has no common sense or that they have no knowledge about child rearing.

5. Be polite. When you meet each other, be courteous and pleasant, and watch your body language. Know that you are creating an example for the children and that they are watching.
6. Encourage the biological parent to take charge. The new partner should play no part in discipline. The biological parent needs to take the lead and be involved. This will help the adults get along and will diminish problems.
7. Attempt to work out differences. This may seem an impossibility at first. You do not need to be best friends, just be civil to one another. The children will be the winners.
8. Be aware of and sensitive to adolescents' perceptions regarding their parents' sexuality. Most children tend to see their parents as nonsexual. Displays of romantic affection are highly uncomfortable for children.
9. Be aware that, as the noncustodial parent, your children have missed you and are greedy for your attention, and it is difficult for them to share you with another adult.
10. Don't try to merge your children with your partner's children until marriage is imminent. Then, allow all the children plenty of time to get to know one another, adjust to the new situation or living arrangements, and get used to the new circumstances.

Ten

New Marriages and Problems Inherent in Them

Taking a new step, uttering a new word,
is what people fear the most.

—Fyodor Dostoevsky

Success is not final, failure is not fatal;
it is the courage to continue that counts.

—Winston Churchill

"Although social pressures encourage stepfamilies' blending, only one out of three stepfamilies survive."[1] Many issues present when families blend: jealousy, competition, feelings of displacement, melding of partner's children, and ex-spouse's reactions. For example, after spending a weekend with the noncustodial parent, the children knows they cannot return to Mommy or Daddy and say they had a great time. Children may feel they are being disloyal to the biological parent if they show affection or goodwill to a new partner or to a stepparent.

Children are often fearful or reluctant to tell one parent that they enjoy the time with the other parent. They are apprehensive that this information potentially can make their parents feel sad, angry, or left out. A nine-year-old boy illustrated this in a drawing. A child of divorce, he was asked to draw a picture of his family. He drew a picture of acrobats balancing on the shoulders of one other. He drew himself in the middle, between his parents, precariously and awkwardly leaning to one side as if he were about to fall over. In the drawing, the child was trying to balance everyone: he felt responsible for keeping his family safe from falling. Children feel helpless and off balance because they cannot fix a situation they did not create.

The best solution for parents is not necessarily the best for children. The impact of divorce can last a lifetime and cause permanent changes to a child's personality, leaving the child with problems ranging from difficulty with intimacy to a lack of trust to a generally more pessimistic view of the world. According to Paulina Kernberg, the second worst trauma a child can experience, after the death of a parent, is divorce.[2] The article goes on to point out that, according to professionals, "conflict is the norm rather than the exception . . . jealousies, divided loyalties, problems with the ex and lingering hurt often combine to turn blended households into battlegrounds." All of these difficulties can potentially erode a new relationship.

Although there are varied reactions to parental remarriage, a considerable number of children initially experience the remarriage of their parents as difficult. Some youngsters exhibit remarkable resilience; other children suffer developmental delays or disruptions. Still others seem to adapt well initially but show delayed reactions that emerge at a later time, especially in adolescence. The long-term effects are related to the child's developmental status, sex, temperament, the qualities of the home and parenting environments, and to the resources and support systems available to the child.

Patrick, now in his fifties, describes how he experienced his mother's remarriage.

> I was the Prince until I was six years old. I was the only grandchild, feted and fussed over by all four grandparents. Everything I did or said was applauded. Then, at age six, my mother filed for divorce, and my world crashed. Suddenly, I was without my father and instead had to adapt to her new boyfriend, who ridiculed me and later physically beat me up on a regular basis.
>
> My relationship with my father and paternal grandparents changed because I was always being instructed to withhold information from them. "Don't tell them" was a constant refrain. It made the relationship awkward and strained.
>
> The divorce was to be final the November after I turned seven. A few months before the divorce, my mother and her soon-to-be husband had a baby girl. I don't remember much about that, but I do remember being very involved with Superman and his powers. A month before the divorce and remarriage, I remember running across a very busy street with my arms held up as if I was flying. I was hit by a car and hospitalized with a bad concussion. I don't remember being hit, I just remember coming to in a hospital bed, and my dad was sitting there looking very upset. He had a big, blue toy Oldsmobile on his lap. Did I run across the street thinking I was Superman

> and invincible? Or was I trying to get their attention to how painful all of this was to me? Did I want to die?

Brett, an only child, was 18 when his mother remarried. To his mother's delight, he had been accepted to a prestigious East Coast college.

> I was her pride and joy. She spent my freshman year bragging to anyone who would listen about me being the only one in my high school to have been accepted there. In the spring of my freshman year, she remarried. She turned my bedroom into a study/den for my stepfather. It felt like there was no longer a place for me. At the end of the year, I dropped out of college. It devastated her. I realize now I was getting even. I joined the military: something unacceptable and upsetting to a woman like my mother. When I worked out my hurt and anger, I was able to return to college and graduated cum laude. Years later I even came to like my stepfather.

The son of a politician revealed that he had been estranged from his father, because he had a "little problem" with his new stepmother. The politician, in speaking of the difficulties between his current wife and his children from a previous marriage, "tapped into the struggles of millions of American families who have to regroup when a new marriage . . . follows a divorce."[3]

ANNOUNCING REMARRIAGE

To protect children and not parade new relationships that may not work out, parents have to be reticent about introductions, think through situations, and use common sense and sensitivity. Once parents have made a decision to remarry, they should develop a strategy ahead of time for how to tell the children. This should be done in stages, starting with an introduction and gradually allowing the children to get to know the person and understand the parent's deepening feelings toward that person. The idea of remarriage should not come as an abrupt shock to children, as described in the following story.

> One day, she announced, "I am getting married in two weeks." Do you believe, she was getting married to this guy we had never even met? We didn't even know he existed. We didn't even know she was dating. My brothers and I were in absolute shock; we were still recovering from the divorce. Apparently, he lived in another city, and, since she traveled a lot for her work, we were unaware of their relationship. We were blown away. She set it up so we hated him from the start. I'm sure that was not her

intention. But that was the result of her behavior. She was a good mother, and I think she thought she was protecting us, but it backfired.

MELDING OF FAMILIES

Even in situations where the remarriage is not a shock, children can feel marginalized by the remarriage.

Dr. L.,

You were right. This was not a good idea. I arrived in California a couple of weeks ago. And at first I was thrilled to be away from Chicago in January, but—and it is a big but—living with my father and stepmother is a nightmare. My stepmother is controlling and just a witch. There are two sets of rules: one for me and one for her own son, who is close in age to me. Let me give you an example. My stepmother has a skin problem, no big whup. She uses it as an excuse for everything. The other day, I went to take a shower in her bathroom, since the hall bath only has a tub. She had a fit and insisted that I would just have to learn to take a bath since her bathroom was off limits because of her skin problem. Later, I found out that her beloved son showers in her bathroom all of the time. I spoke to Dad and he did not want to get involved and kind of told me to just cool it, there was nothing he could do. So, Dr. L., what do I do? I don't have the money to move out. Do I confront her? Of course, I may be wrong, but I do not think my dad is going to go to the mat for me. He will not put his relationship with her on the line for me.

HELP!

Sam

Sam,

Nice to hear from you. Wish the circumstances were better.

As a freshman you really need to concentrate on your college courses and cannot take a full-time job in order to support your moving out of your dad's house. You are in a very difficult position. Your dad clearly will not stick his neck out for you. That is something you are going to have to adjust to and accept.

You and I talked about your dad's passivity and inability to stand up for you at the expense of his marriage. Perhaps you could ask for a family dinner where you could raise the question of different rules for different sons. Ask for some clarification. You do run the risk of making her angry, and she may be punitive as a result. You are working on your voice, not her hearing. Let me know how it turns out.

Regards,

The issue of stepchildren is fraught with difficulties. Each partner has to decide on his or her priority—the marriage or the biological child. This can result in arguments, guilt, internal struggles, anxiety, frustration, anger, and tension. Having suffered from a failed marriage, the parent is often reluctant to replicate conflict of any kind. It is no wonder that only one in three stepfamilies survive. The best solution for parents is not necessarily the best solution for the child.

When a stepparent disapproves of the biological parent's behavior toward his or her children, this can put a strain on the relationship and can result in divisiveness and arguments. People have different parenting styles and sensibilities. If a couple can communicate, this issue can be overcome. For example, a harsh and unsympathetic father who is critical of a child presents difficulty for a sensitive and empathic woman. Equally, a selfish and manipulative mother creates a problem for a rational man.

Often children are reluctant to report mistreatment by a stepparent for fear of causing a rift or breakup in their parent's new relationship. The children fear they will be responsible for the demise of yet another marriage and so remain silent. Francie, a nine-year-old girl, was reluctant to tell her parents and stepmother about her adolescent stepbrother's inappropriate fondling of her. It was only when it became apparent in dollhouse play in the safety of the therapist's office that the story emerged. When the therapist suggested the inclusion of the parents to discuss the problem, Francie became tearful and upset. "My stepmother will hate me, they'll fight and get divorced and it will all be my fault. And then my mother will yell at my dad and I'll be in the middle again."

For melded families to have a chance of success there has to be good, open communication, understanding, and patience. There also has to be an understanding and awareness of parental instincts: a need to protect one's biological offspring.

Daly and Wilson's research shows that children are statistically at much greater risk of murder or abuse by stepparents than by biological parents.[4] Similarly, Hardy's study illustrates the way dominant male langur monkeys kill the infant offspring of rivals before mating with the infants' mothers.[5] Of course, there are plenty of loving stepparents, but research statistics are sadly on the side of the Cinderella tradition, with its stereotype of the wicked stepmother.

A Wichita, Kansas, newspaper reported a troubling story. Two emaciated sisters were found by state social workers in the basement of their father's home. The six- and seven-year-old girls were severely malnourished. They told police they only received food when their father, a trucker, was at home, which was infrequent. The household had plenty of food, and the stepsiblings were well cared for. A physician told the police it appeared that the girls had not eaten in six days. The physician added, "This is not a six-day starvation, obviously these kids have been starved for quite awhile."[6] This is an extreme example of the Cinderella syndrome. Stepparents may be unsympathetic, but they are usually not destructively brutal.

Blending families when both partners have families of their own can sometimes be difficult. There are issues of competition, jealousy, sadness at being replaced and displaced, and feelings of being left out. One set of children gets to stay, while the others have to leave. "It seemed whenever I had to leave, they were going to do something fun, like have a barbeque or go the movies. I always felt like I was marginalized and left out."

When one set of children is considerably older than the other, blending tends to be more easily accomplished. When children are of the same age or close in age, jealousy and competition are more likely, as described in the following letter and response.

Dear Dr. L.,

I want to ask you a favor. I remember your saying I could write you when I married and moved away.

As you remember, I married a man who has a son who is the same age as Simon. Actually their birthdays are a day apart. Charles (his son) has always been extremely jealous of Simon. When Simon's father bought him a computer, Charles became quite hysterical, weeping and carrying on until my husband agreed to buy him one. If Simon went on a trip with us, Charles would beg and get his father to agree to take him somewhere "because Simon went," despite the fact that their school vacation schedules were different. I don't know what to do; suggestions?

Best,

Clare

Dear Clare,

Blending families is difficult. There is often competition between the children. They bring a host of feelings resulting from the divorce to the new situation. It has to be difficult for Charles seeing his dad spending so much time with Simon, who is the same age as he is, when he only gets every other weekend with his dad. The issue is not the computer or the trip, but what these things represent. To give in to Charles's demands will not solve the problem. It will only ratchet up the demands, because they are being reinforced. Your husband really needs to sit down with Charles and address the real issues with him. He needs to tell him that he understands how difficult the situation is for Charles. The two of them need to spend "special time" together—time when it is the just the two of them. Another suggestion is that the four of you attend a few sessions with a family therapist, and some of these issues could be hashed out.

Nice to hear from you.

Jealousy and competition between biological children and a stepparent or partner are another possibility. Children who are vulnerable from the effects of the divorce may view a stepparent as a threat to their relationship with their parent. In a divorce situation, children no longer have access to both parents all the time, so the time becomes precious with each parent, and there may be a reluctance to share that time with "an outsider." Feeling threatened and dealing with a sense of loss perpetuated by the divorce, children may need total affection, which they are resentful of sharing. To avoid this, the new person should be introduced gradually and slowly, in small doses. As previously stated, sensitivity and patience are essential.

On the other hand, stepparents are sometimes competitive with, or jealous of, stepchildren. They may resent the time dedicated to the children, the parent's involvement with the children, and the money spent on the children. The residue of a life spent with someone else is sometimes too explicit a memory for the new partner. Or personality issues and issues from their own background may contribute to these feelings.

Patrick, an only child, was five when his parents divorced. His mother remarried very shortly thereafter to a man who was not of the same social or educational background as Patrick's father. The stepfather mocked and demeaned Patrick incessantly and was physically abusive to Patrick, resulting in a hospitalization when Patrick was 17 years old. He broke all of Patrick's fingers and beat him so severely around the head and back that it caused a severe concussion. Despite fathering six children of his own, his jealousy of Patrick and what he represented never abated. Patrick's mother, financially dependent on the stepfather and now with six children, turned a blind eye to the abuse of her son and the pain inflicted on him by the stepfather. At the age of 55, Patrick is still dealing with the residual emotions.

Even when the new stepparent is aware of these feelings, they have difficulty dealing with them, as the following letter discloses.

Dr. L.,

I've done it again, I just can't control myself. You know I really hate his kids. Well, the daughter came down to visit us in Palm Beach and I ended up blasting her; that she was a selfish young woman who was just interested in her father's money. Of course, I should never have told her of the sweet 16 bash we threw for our daughter at the country club and the zippy sports car we gave her. That got her going, and she tearfully said her father never gave her a sweet 16, never mind the present. Then we were into it. She reminded me of how I stole her father from her mother and broke up their family. Now what do I do?

As you know, my husband stays out of it and he is no help in this sort of situation. I need your help desperately!

Meg

Dear Meg,

Well, you're right. You did it again. You have to wonder why you cannot control yourself around Stephanie and why you need to promote your daughter all the time, knowing that it will provoke an outburst with your stepdaughter. After all, you are the adult. It seems that you have competitive feelings toward Stephanie. This is something we need to explore when you return. Why do you need to do this? Does she remind you of Hattie, your younger sister? Why do you need to constantly put her in her place? What is it about her that sets you off? These are questions that we need to explore further once you get back to town.

Regards,

The following letter is a good example of the difficulties encountered between couples who are considering melding their families.

Dr. L.,

I want to give you some background before we meet on Tuesday. I don't want to forget any of this. This may sound mean, but, quite honestly, I hate her kid. He's a 10-year-old brat, spoiled, whiny, and totally uninterested in any sport. And you know how I feel about sports! This kid will not even throw a ball with me. Everything he says or does irritates me. I am not crazy about her daughter either, but she is more palatable. The problem is, I'm crazy about the mother, and we are supposed to get married next month. After all, the kid will leave for college in eight years. Can I last that long? I know we will talk about this on Tuesday. Just a heads up.

Paul

Perhaps Paul needs to consider the child's interest instead of his own. To form a good relationship with the child, he needs to understand that the child may be suffering from the effects of his parent's divorce; he may be as unhappy with Paul as Paul is with him. Just because the boy does not enjoy the same sporting activities as Paul does not make him a bad kid. He may be terribly upset at his mother's possible new alliance. Paul, as the adult, needs to try to reach out to the child, find some area of common interest with him, and build a relationship with him.

The pain that a stepparent can inadvertently cause is evident in the following quote.

> My parents were divorced when I was an infant, and my father brought me to this country when he immigrated. Several years later, he married an American woman with a child of her own. When I was about eight years old, I overheard a telephone conversation in which she was telling her sister that she was leaving my father because of the constant fighting over money. When she hung up the phone, she realized I had heard the conversation. She swung around and barked, "And don't ever call me Mommy, I am not your mother."

A stepparent's jealousy and dislike may take a tragic turn. Joan was consumed by jealousy, particularly of her stepson. Her husband had been previously married and had a child, Teddy, from that marriage. Joan deliberately made the child unwelcome when he visited, constantly criticizing him, demeaning him, and making him feel inadequate. Only Teddy's tears would temporarily lessen her attacks. His father, a passive man, did not stand up to his wife and did nothing to protect his son despite his love for the child. After a year or two, Teddy begged not to have to visit. Thereafter, he saw his father rarely. At the age of 12, Teddy visited his father one last time. After one of his stepmother's tirades against him, he went for a bike ride in the neighborhood. He was struck by a car and died on impact.

BIRTH OF NEW CHILDREN: "OUR CHILDREN" VERSUS "MY CHILDREN"

With the birth of a child from a new union, difficulties should be anticipated. When one does not think ahead, trouble looms. Unrealistic expectations sometimes can be naïve. "They will all love the baby and be so excited." Not necessarily.

When Meg and her new husband had their child, the reaction of his older children from his first marriage was not one of excitement or love. They were jealous, fearful of being displaced, and angry at being replaced. Their biological mother, still reeling from her husband's affair and subsequent remarriage, fueled the fires. The older children never adjusted to their father's attachment to the baby. Many years later, the oldest daughter baked a birthday cake for Lacy, the younger daughter. Lacy had a late October birthday. Stephanie decorated the cake with tombstones and festooned the cake with "rest in peace," ostensibly in recognition of Halloween. This was her thinly disguised wish to eliminate Lacy.

It is imperative that parents have an awareness of and sensitivity to the impact of a divorce, a remarriage, and a new baby. Biological parents, despite their ex's reaction to the birth of a new child, need to set a tone of acceptance and love for the new baby who is now a part of the family.

There are situations, particularly when there is big age difference, where there is genuine love for the new baby. "I remember my father telling us, 'I want you to accept and love Bill as your brother, not as your stepbrother.' And we did."

EX-SPOUSE'S REACTION TO A NEW MARRIAGE

Ex-spouses can have complicated reactions when their former partner remarries. The reaction depends on the length of time since the divorce, the current circumstances of their life, and their own feelings of contentment. It is usually difficult to feel that one has been replaced, especially if one has not remarried, if the ex-spouse married the person responsible for the breakup of the marriage, and when there are financial consequences.

When ex-spouses or their extended family are angry or bitter, they may use the children as a vehicle for acting out their frustrations. The following two cases describe how the result of such behavior can be quite destructive.

> Sometimes, I wonder if my mom didn't have her own agenda when she forbade him from seeing me. I know he disappointed me repeatedly by not showing up. But then I have to wonder. You know, he did marry her closest girlfriend, and I'm sure she had feelings about that. She felt so betrayed by both of them. Maybe she used me as a way of getting back at him.
>
> I feel like an only child. It really is a burden, especially now that he is in his eighties and not well. His daughters are the same ages as my mom, and they will have nothing to do with him. So I am the one who carries the burden of getting him to doctors' appointments and helping him financially. I think his daughters' not talking to him originally was the result of his first wife's manipulations. I know she was furious when he married someone the same age as their daughters.
>
> I've never even met my half sisters. As a child, I felt so badly about it. I felt there was something wrong with me. My parents sent me to therapy

because my self-esteem was so poor. I felt they did not want to talk to my dad because of me. His first wife punished all of us. I wonder if she realized what she was doing.

My mom keeps telling us we would not be in this position if Dad hadn't left us. He didn't leave us, he left her. But that's her constant song. She's really punishing us. She quit her job, took to her bed, and just lazes around and says terrible things about Dad. She is always screaming at us to get money from Dad, even for piddly stuff, like bus fare. She does not realize how hurtful it is to us. We miss him. We miss being a family and it's so painful—all the nasty things she says about him. After all, he's our dad. We love him, and we don't dislike Val, his new wife.

GOLDEN RULES

1. Prepare children well in advance for the new marriage.
2. Help children in their confusion and anger about the changes that are occurring in their family.
3. Encourage children to talk about their feelings of rivalry or unhappiness by talking with them. Listen to them, and spend time alone with each child. Younger children may have an easier time expressing their feelings than older children.
4. Take your children's questions and concerns seriously and listen to what they say. A child needs to be heard, regardless of age.
5. Some children engage in conflict because they are competing for their parents' attention.
6. Expect children (no matter what their age) to have a reaction to this dramatic change in their lives.
7. Reassure your children that you love them and always will.

Appendix A: Golden Rules

CHAPTER ONE

1. Think over the decision to divorce very carefully. Romance, excitement, and passion do not necessarily last. There need to be very real reasons for a divorce. Many lives will be altered, and divorce affects children for the rest of their lives.
2. Before rushing for a divorce, it is wise to try couples therapy.
3. Reach out for help for the children. Often children of divorcing parents are angry or scared, and they need help with understanding their feelings. If they misbehave, they may need some help in expressing their feelings with words rather than through behaviors. An objective, trained third party may be the answer.
4. Be aware of your own needs. Many parents who are in the throes of a divorce are so involved with helping everyone else through the divorce that they forget about themselves. If necessary, seek help for yourself with a trained professional or reach out to friends and family.
5. Examine and be honest with yourself. Is the cause of your unhappiness your marriage, or is it something else?
6. Don't rush into the decision to divorce. Maintain flexibility and an open mind. What looks like a problem today may not be viewed as a serious problem in the future. Listen to your inner feelings. Consider what attracted you to the person in the first place, and explain to yourself what happened to this attraction.
7. Consider what your life will be like without your spouse. There are financial and social consequences.

8. Be practical. The divorce process is not as easy as you might think. There are often battles over child custody, property, pensions, temporary financial support, and taxation.
9. Do not glamorize the single existence. Are you prepared to be a single parent, assuming much more responsibility for caring for children on a daily basis?
10. Be honest about how you contribute to the difficulties you are experiencing.
11. Make up your own mind. Do not let others influence you and so determine the future of your marriage.
12. Divorce is forever. Remember, once you are divorced, it is difficult to undo.
13. Think before you act. Think about the impact of divorce on your immediate and extended family.

CHAPTER TWO

1. Tell your children why (if appropriate) you are divorcing. Give them a reason that is easy to understand. Try to tell them when the whole family (including both spouses and all children) is together.
2. Be available to listen.
3. Reassure your children that the divorce is not their fault.
4. Tell the truth to your children so as not to fuel expectations about a possible reunion. Gently remind children that the divorce is final and that you will not get back together. If children are to learn to trust, the truth must always be told. Every time children are told an untruth, we carve away at their ability to trust.
5. Do not dismiss children's perceptions of events, because this can cause children to doubt their own observations and judgments.
6. Do not provide too many details that will overwhelm the children.
7. Don't hide your emotions. Children should know you feel sad over the loss. It gives children permission to express their sadness. Never say "Don't feel scared or sad."
8. Use age-appropriate language.
9. Remind children that both parents love them.
10. Encourage discussions with children about their thoughts and feelings; be sensitive to children's fears.
11. Use a calendar to show young children when they will see the noncustodial parent. Very young children have little concept of time. Reassuring children that they will see the parent "next Sunday" has little meaning for them, but showing the days on a calendar can help.
12. Transitional objects are useful for young children. Following a divorce or separation, young children may be fearful of abandonment. A transitional object, such as a favorite teddy bear or blanket, can offer comfort and be reassuring to the child.

13. Avoid drama. Talk to the children when you are calm.
14. Try to keep conversations neutral and nonblaming.
15. Be patient.
16. Try to limit the damage caused by divorce.

CHAPTER THREE

1. Talk about the move or the splitting up of the household.
2. Help the children anticipate the change.
3. Maintain relationships and routines. Consistency and stability are of paramount importance. Time spent with each parent has changed. Emotions are in turmoil, and living arrangements are initially confusing, so it is vital that as much constancy as possible be maintained. Preserve as many routines of your child's former life as possible. Keep up relationships with grandparents, aunts and uncles, neighbors, and friends.
4. Stay calm on moving day.
5. Children should not witness the actual moving out.
6. Be aware that children are particularly emotionally vulnerable at this time.
7. Pay attention to the moods of your children.
8. When a parent moves out of the family home, the children may appear to be unaffected; however, there is always an underlying emotional reaction.
9. Monitor your own behavior carefully. Try to shield your children from your stress.
10. Try to minimize the changes that divorce brings. For example, try to keep children in the same school, the same home, and involved in the same activities.

CHAPTER FOUR

1. The best interests of the children are of crucial consideration. Custody fights can be extremely detrimental to both adults and children. Parents are encouraged to try and work out arrangements regarding the children out of court.
2. Try to be reasonable and flexible. Do not react out of anger and spite. The children suffer when this happens.
3. The children's well-being is crucial. Do not use a custody fight to express your anger and bitterness.
4. Remind yourself of the King Solomon story. Children cannot be cut in half; find a workable and fair solution that keeps the children very much intact.
5. Avoid engaging in conflicts. Research concludes that emotional and behavioral problems are more frequent in high-conflict situations.
6. Parents who share custody are encouraged to establish schedules. This gives children a feeling of stability.

7. If you are the parent who pays child support, do not let your children suffer economically by withholding child support.
8. If you are the noncustodial parent, remain involved with your children, seeing them often. Frequency and regularity of visits affect self-esteem and behaviors.
9. Attempt to work out a custody agreement amicably. Custody battles are financially and emotionally costly, and the consequences can be devastating.
10. Make every attempt to keep children with their siblings.

CHAPTER FIVE

1. Children need both parents in their lives.
2. Don't give up being a part of your children's lives. Remember, children thrive with two parents. Even if you're not living with your children or are separated by distance, there are ways you can be involved and interested in your children's daily existence.
3. Do not use derogatory language or demean the other parent. Do not use insulting language or say insulting things about the other parent.
4. Consider your children's needs rather than being focused on "winning."
5. Allow your children their right to have a relationship with both parents.
6. Do not deprive your children of a parent no matter how you feel about the other parent. You will be harming your children.
7. Keep your own emotions separate and under control. Your anger, hurt, and dislike are for you to deal with. Don't impose these on your children.
8. Try and be supportive of your children's relationship with the noncustodial parent. It is for your children's good.
9. Do not manipulate or encourage your children to sever their relationship with the other parent.
10. Difficulties your children may encounter with the other parent can be worked through with a trained professional. Supporting alienation is not the answer.
11. Always think of what is best for the children.
12. Think of the future. Alienation from a parent will have long-term effects on your children.
13. Alienation from a parent can be supported only after speaking with a professional who recommends severing the relationship with the parent. Emotional abuse, physical abuse, sexual abuse, parental drug or alcohol addiction, or behaviors that endanger the children's safety are the major reasons for such drastic measures.

CHAPTER SIX

1. The children's needs should be the priority at this difficult time in their life.
2. Don't use the children as weapons against your ex-spouse.
3. Don't use the children as "moles" who are expected to report information. Try not to press them for information about what happened when they were visiting with the other parent. Children usually feel uncomfortable offering information. If they do, listen closely and be supportive.
4. Don't make children choose between parents. Don't make them take sides. Children generally want to make both their parents happy.
5. Don't criticize the other parent in front of the children. Your ex-spouse is still your children's parent; when you criticize the other parent, your children may feel you are criticizing them indirectly.
6. Let your children be children, not your confidants.
7. Respect the other parent's values even if they don't replicate yours.
8. Be dependable. This offers comfort to children during a stressful time.
9. The age and developmental needs of children should be taken into account when helping them deal with this painful and upsetting event.
10. Patience, understanding, and empathy are vital.
11. Keep your own issues separate.
12. Be nonjudgmental with regard to the other parent.
13. Allow and encourage your children to enjoy their other parent.
14. Do not make children keep secrets from the other parent.
15. Do not ever put the children in the middle.

CHAPTER SEVEN

1. No matter how you feel or felt about your former in-laws, remember that grandparents are an important support system for your children.
2. Do not disparage grandparents, uncles, and aunts.
3. Do not withhold visits with grandparents.
4. Permit continued relationships with grandparents.
5. Do not deprive children of grandparents who add richness to children's lives.
6. Do not inflict another loss on children by depriving them of their grandparents.
7. When a decision is made to divorce, decide how to tell friends and extended family, how much to say, and who should tell whom.
8. If you are the grandparent, try to remain in a cordial relationship with your former son- or daughter-in-law. This is in the best interest of your grandchildren.

9. If you are the grandparent, do not attempt to get your grandchildren to take sides or to influence them against the other parent.
10. If you are the grandparent, try to be flexible, and keep the children's best interests as your priority, which may mean initially seeing your grandchildren less often or for shorter visits. Be patient—it will lead to a better and more healthy outcome for the grandchildren.
11. If you are the grandparent, do not demean your former daughter- or son-in-law. This is a parent whom the child loves, and it will be hurtful and destructive to the child.

CHAPTER EIGHT

1. Be aware that the changes in roles are difficult for everyone in the family. Time to adjust is needed.
2. A change in roles and status should not demean self-worth.
3. Be aware that there are many new roles that will have to be learned such as disciplining, communicating, housekeeping, and financial responsibility.
4. Understand that everyone's role in the family has changed.
5. Each partner is now a head of household and needs to assert his or her own authority. Children have to adjust to this change.
6. As decision-making roles change, don't discount your children's point of view.
7. Be upfront with your ex-spouse about changes that the new roles have necessitated.
8. Accept advice regarding negotiating a change in role. Listen and try not to be defensive. But also be discerning about the advice given.
9. Changing roles is a time of learning. One is not expected to know all the answers.
10. Try not to be overwhelmed with all the changes. A little humor helps.

CHAPTER NINE

1. Do not introduce every new boyfriend or girlfriend to the children. Only introduce people when the relationship is serious.
2. Talk to children about a new relationship ahead of time.
3. Avoid competition. If you are the ex-spouse, keep in mind that it is helpful for your children to have one more encouraging, loving adult in their life. Try to avoid thinking of them as the new spouse, and regard them as someone who is potentially important to your children.

   If you are the stepmother, let the children's mother know that you do not want to replace her, you want to help take care of the children. Ask her for schedules and special accommodations that the children might require.

4. Do not automatically regard the new partner as an adversary. Do not assume that the stepparent has no common sense or that they have no knowledge about child rearing.
5. Be polite. When you meet each other, be courteous and pleasant, and watch your body language. Know that you are creating an example for the children and that they are watching.
6. Encourage the biological parent to take charge. The new partner should play no part in discipline. The biological parent needs to take the lead and be involved. This will help the adults get along and will diminish problems.
7. Attempt to work out differences. This may seem an impossibility at first. You do not need to be best friends, just be civil to one another. The children will be the winners.
8. Be aware of and sensitive to adolescents' perceptions regarding their parents' sexuality. Most children tend to see their parents as nonsexual. Displays of romantic affection are highly uncomfortable for children.
9. Be aware that, as the noncustodial parent, your children have missed you and are greedy for your attention, and it is difficult for them to share you with another adult.
10. Don't try to merge your children with your partner's children until marriage is imminent. Then, allow all the children plenty of time to get to know one another, adjust to the new situation or living arrangements, and get used to the new circumstances.

CHAPTER TEN

1. Prepare children well in advance for the new marriage.
2. Help children in their confusion and anger about the changes that are occurring in their family.
3. Encourage children to talk about their feelings of rivalry or unhappiness by talking with them. Listen to them, and spend time alone with each child. Younger children may have an easier time expressing their feelings than older children.
4. Take your children's questions and concerns seriously and listen to what they say. A child needs to be heard, regardless of age.
5. Some children engage in conflict because they are competing for their parents' attention.
6. Expect children (no matter what their age) to have a reaction to this dramatic change in their lives.
7. Reassure your children that you love them and always will.

Appendix B: As Marriage and Parenthood Drift Apart, Public Is Concerned about Social Impact—Generation Gap in Values, Behaviors, July 1, 2007

In 2007, the Pew Research Center conducted a telephone survey of 2,020 randomly selected adults ages 18 to 49. Some of the interesting findings are summarized below:

- The survey found that Americans consider marriage to be an important goal and component of their lives.
- Americans' definition of a successful marriage continues to change over time.
- Marriage in the early twenty-first century has less influence on how people arrange their lives and on their decisions about having and raising children than at any other time in U.S. history.
- Married people are more satisfied with their lives than unmarried adults.
- Divorce is preferable to remaining in a bad marriage.
- More Americans agree with the statement that "divorce is painful, but preferable to maintaining an unhappy marriage." People tended to think that children are better off if the parents get divorced than they are if the parents stay together unhappily.
- People who were polled do not agree with the statement, "divorce should be avoided except in an extreme situation."
- In the 1990s, when the U.S. public was asked to rank (on a World Values Survey) how important children were to a marriage, children ranked third in importance. In the 2007 Pew survey, children ranked eighth

(out of nine) in importance to a successful marriage—ranking below sharing household chores, good housing, adequate income, happy sexual relationship, and faithfulness.

- Most people feel that the main purpose of marriage is the mutual happiness and fulfillment of the couple rather than the bearing and rearing of children. Children do, however, remain central to a parent's personal happiness. Children occupy a pedestal matched only by a person's relationship with his or her spouse.

Appendix C: Financial Aspects of Divorce

Authors Lewis and Lippman are qualified to address the many emotional issues involved in divorce. However, since neither of them has relevant credentials, expertise, or experience in the area of finance or economics, they approached the subject of this appendix, the financial aspects of divorce, with considerable trepidation. That said, they quickly realized that their relative naïveté was actually an asset because it forced them to acknowledge that the best advice they could give to readers would be to seek out appropriate legal and financial guidance. So, rather than presume to offer financial guidance to readers, they followed their own counsel and sought the advice of a financial planner.

This appendix will (1) provide you with suggestions about where to find expert guidance, (2) familiarize you with some of the general principles of financial planning, and (3) mention some examples from the financial planner's personal experience that might provide useful and cautionary tales.

Naturally, the first step in making sure that a divorce does not cause unnecessary economic hardship is to find a good lawyer who specializes in divorce. While lawyers who help sell your house or help you write your will might be excellent resources in their particular fields, they are unlikely to be familiar with all of the issues and nuances of marital law. An excellent first step in finding a matrimonial lawyer is to contact the American Academy of Matrimonial Lawyers at (312) 263-6477 or use its search function at http://www.aaml.org/custom/directory/search.cfm.

You should also consult your friends who have gone through a divorce because they may be a valuable source. Once you have made a list of names in your area,

---

This appendix was written by a certified financial planner.

you should (1) contact your local bar association to see if any of the lawyers on your list have ever been subject to disciplinary proceedings, (2) review their credentials on a legal Web site such as MartindaleHubble.com (which also allows you to search for lawyers who specialize in family law), and (3) interview at least three of the lawyers to determine whether their fees, skills, and personality are a good fit for your situation.

While it remains your lawyer's job to make sure that you get all the economic benefits to which you are legally entitled, not every divorce lawyer is familiar with the intricacies of the securities markets and the tax code. Similarly, not every divorce lawyer understands how to calculate the present value of a spouse's future earnings stream, can readily value nonqualified deferred compensation, or provide an appropriate value for a closely held corporation. So, in addition to obtaining appropriate legal representation, persons seeking a divorce—particularly higher–net worth individuals—should be certain to retain the services of an appropriate financial professional. Unfortunately, determining which kind of financial professional will be most helpful is not always easy. Consider beginning your search with a certified financial planner. CFPs can be found both by referral and by going to http://www.cfpboard.org/search. Even if a CFP is unable to provide the full panoply of expertise needed for a complicated financial situation, he or she is likely to have working relationships with certified public accountants, certified divorce mediators (CDMAs), appraisers, credit counselors, bankers, mortgage brokers, insurance agents, and financial advisors who have the requisite knowledge and skills to provide sound counsel.

Although it is imperative that persons going through a divorce have access to the guidance of experts, such guidance seldom comes cheaply. To minimize the cost of ensuring an equitable distribution of assets, liabilities, and future economic costs and benefits, you must organize your facts and your questions prior to your appointments with your lawyer and your financial planner. Understandably, this is also one of the ground rules for working with many financial planners.

For people who need help in organizing themselves prior to their meetings, consider asking the advisor if his or her firm has prepared financial data forms, or use the forms available at http://nolo.com/resource.cfm/catID/BC93B1DE-97D2–44DB-87F20B0350BA0643/118/246/. In addition, the terminally disorganized should request old tax returns by going to http://irs.gov/ and submitting form 4506-T (Request for Transcript of Tax Returns) and going to http://ssa.gov/ to check their benefits. Everyone should bring copies of their own and their spouse's pay stubs, deeds, brokerage accounts, 401(k)s, 403(b)s, 457s, pensions, nonqualified deferred compensation, all debts (especially mortgage, home equity, margin, and credit card debt), copies of all insurance policies, copies of a typical month's expenditures (broken down by person), copies of all other assets, copies of all wills, powers of attorney, advanced health care directives, trusts, articles of incorporation, partnership agreements, and all other financial facts to your meetings with both your prospective financial advisor and your lawyer. By not forcing your advisors to find and organize your information for you, you may be able to reduce the number of billable hours for which you must pay.

In addition to having all of your factual information organized and with you when you meet with prospective advisors, another basic rule of financial planning is that you should immediately inform your financial advisor and lawyer of any special circumstances that you feel make your position unique. For example, your individual situation can differ from the norm for reasons that vary from being an emergency room physician (who will probably be unable to work in that capacity beyond the age of 55) to having a child who is disabled and will need a lifetime of care and support. Don't expect a financial planner or lawyer to be a mind reader or an expert on everything. If some of the facts of your life make your situation different from that of the run-of-the-mill divorcing person, you must inform both your lawyer and financial advisor in your first meeting. With that knowledge, he or she will hopefully be able to both provide you with good advice and inform your other advisors (with your permission) that there are exceptional aspects to your case that need to be evaluated prior to any settlement.

A third rule of financial planning that has particular relevance for divorcing persons is the need to determine how much you need to save and invest each month, particularly given the pervasive tendency of Americans to save insufficiently for future goals. Since many articles have noted (and decried) the society-wide lack of savings and the U.S. Department of Commerce's Bureau of Economic Analysis has found that the average personal savings rate for Americans has averaged less than 2 percent over the last seven years (http://www.bea.gov/briefrm/saving.htm), the apportionment of financial responsibilities in a divorce makes a concomitant understanding of the necessary savings and investment strategies essential. For example, if one of the parties to a divorce agrees to pay for the education of two teenage children through law school at the alma mater of both parents (a private institution), someone needs to perform what financial advisors call the "Texas Three-Step." In other words, given the historical rate of inflation for private educational institutions, the likely rate of return on investments, and the amount of time remaining before educational bills come due, how much does the responsible parent need to set aside each month to have a reasonable expectation of paying for the legal obligation to educate their children at their alma mater? Similarly, when spouses who didn't deal with money matters are suddenly handed responsibility for their own financial life, they need to have an expert present a written financial plan detailing how much they need to save each month into which investments in order to be on track for the retirement they envisage. Naturally, it behooves all persons who are divorcing to pay for this type of analysis prior to any final agreement, because they either need to be certain that the agreement provides them with the means to address their financial needs or they need to reconsider the financial viability of that agreement. Conceivably, when confronted with the financial implications of a divorce, couples might even decide to remain married.

Obviously, every person contemplating a divorce should act mainly based on the advice of the qualified advisors whom they are paying. Nonetheless, financial professionals have observed certain patterns in divorce that may be of interest to a broad lay audience. Most notably, they have observed that men tend to leave a divorce in better financial shape than women do. That this is so is also attested to by general media sources. While the author in no way wishes to undermine the recommendations of the professionals you are using, he remains acutely cognizant of the fact that many women who have presumably used well-qualified professionals have left a marriage in worse economic shape—despite the fact that qualified lawyers presumably guided them. The lesson for women seems inescapable: hiring a good lawyer simply isn't good enough. Make sure your lawyer is committed to fighting for you.

Another pattern that many financial advisors believe recurs frequently is that women who opt to use a mediator rather than the traditional "adversarial" system (of two lawyers each seeking to protect his or her client's interests) tend to receive relatively poor financial settlements. While these anecdotal observations are disputed by some of the literature—most notably the Divorce Mediation Center, http://www.divorceresourcecenter.com/Divorce_Information/Divorce_Mediation—the perception is so uniform among financial advisors that mediation tends to favor men that any woman thinking of using mediation should consult with at least two lawyers prior to making such an unconventional decision. Naturally, anyone thinking of agreeing to a settlement needs to have that settlement reviewed by both a divorce lawyer and an appropriate financial advisor prior to signing it.

While the skepticism voiced in the previous paragraph toward divorce mediation might seem peculiar given some of the primary authors' other comments about it, the following example, recently encountered by this appendix's author, illustrates some of the pitfalls of eschewing the guidance of traditional legal counsel in favor of a mediator. (To protect the anonymity of the client on whom this example is based, certain biographical and chronological details have been deliberately altered.)

A Danish woman in her late thirties retained an advisor to perform an analysis so that she could appropriately invest a sizable bequest from her (still-living) father. During the data gathering meeting, it quickly became apparent that the divorce mediator who handled her extraordinarily amicable divorce based many of his recommendations on the assumption that such an attractive woman would quickly marry a rich man and that the woman's father, a wealthy executive who was in his seventies, would leave her a substantial inheritance. Because the woman was fully cognizant of her father's wealth and was exceptionally keen to have a speedy resolution to the process (both because she wanted to spare her daughters a prolonged conflict and because she found the haggling deeply distasteful), she agreed to a settlement that provided her with many of the marital assets but no dependable source of income. Further, she agreed to pay for her daughters' college education, forgo any share of her husband's pension, forfeit any right to alimony, and absorb many of the costs associated with their daughters' equestrian competitions.

The mediator had, by his own lights, done his job exceptionally well. He had minimized the conflict in an inherently conflict-filled process. He had done so by essentially having one of his clients give everything away. Unfortunately, this didn't occur to one of his clients either. Clearly, many mediators are more savvy, but, before signing an agreement that can have lifelong consequences, doesn't it make sense to have both a lawyer and a financial advisor review the settlement first? After all, most wars would end quickly if one side simply surrendered.

Notes

CHAPTER ONE

1. Adapted from Friends in Recovery staff, *The Twelve Steps for Adult Children* (San Diego: RPI Publishing, 1996).

CHAPTER THREE

1. It is estimated that as many as one in five children and adolescents may have a mental health disorder that can be identified and require treatment. *Mental Health: A Report of the Surgeon General* (Rockville, MD: U.S. Department of Health and Human Services, 1999). Other statistics from this source indicate that

- An estimated two-thirds of all young people with mental health problems are not getting the help they need.
- Studies indicate that one in five children and adolescents may have a diagnosable disorder. Estimates of the number of children in the United States who have mental disorders range from 7.7 million to 12.8 million.

Brief Notes on the Mental Health of Children and Adolescents (Bethesda, MD: National Institutes of Health, 1999), http://www.nimh.nih.gov. *Fact Sheet: Going to Extremes, Bipolar Disorder* (Bethesda, MD: National Institutes of Health, 2001). *Press Release: Progressive Brain Changes Detected in Child Onset Schizophrenia* (Bethesda, MD: National Institutes of Health, 1997).

CHAPTER FOUR

1. E. M. Hetherington and J. D. Arasteh, eds., *Custody of Children Following Divorce: Impact of Divorce, Single Parenting and Step-parenting on Children* (Hillsdale, NJ: Lawrence Erlbaum, 1988).

2. Leslie Kaufman, "In Custody Fights, A Hurdle for the Poor," *New York Times*, April 8, 2007, 21.

3. Tom Davies, "Plane Crash into House Followed Bitter Divorce," *Seattle Post-Intelligencer*, http://seattletimes.nwsource.com/html/nationworld/2003604952_crash07.html.

4. Perrine Stephen, "Keeping Divorced Dads at a Distance," *New York Times*, June 18, 2006.

5. Associated Press Writer Tom Murphy in Indianapolis contributed to this report. "Man Flies Plane into Mother-in-Law's House," Associated Press, March 6, 2007.

6. Sanfold L. Braver, Ira M. Ellman, and William V. Fabricus, "Relocation of Children after Divorce and Children's Best Interests: New Evidence and Legal Considerations," *Journal of Family Psychology* 17, no. 2 (2003): 206–19.

7. Ibid.

CHAPTER SIX

1. Bruno Bettelheim, *The Columbia World of Quotations*. Ed. Robert Andrews, Mary Biggs, and Michael Seidel. New York: Columbia University Press, 2006. eNotes.com, 2006. Available at http://www.enotes.com/famous-quotes/most-advice-on-child-rearing-is-sought-in-the-hope. Accessed January 19, 2008.

2. Patrick F. Fagan and Robert E. Rector, "The Effects of Divorce on America," available at http://www.heritage.org/Research/Family/BG1373.cfm.

3. StoryCorps, Library of Congress. Heard on "Morning Edition," National Public Radio, January 27, 2006, available online at http://www.npr.org/templates/story/story.php?storyid=5173527.

CHAPTER EIGHT

1. E. Mark Cummings and Patrick Davies, *Children and Marital Conflict: The Impact of Family Dispute and Resolution* (New York: Guilford Press, 1994).

CHAPTER TEN

1. J. Brooke, "Home Alone Together," *New York Times*, May 4, 2006, D5.

2. Kate S. Lombardi, "Making a Case for Staying Together," *New York Times*, February 4, 2001.

3. M. Navarro, "A Family Feud That Is Familiar," *New York Times*, March 11, 2007.

4. M. Daly and M. Wilson, "Infanticide," in *Parenthood in America: An Encyclopedia*, ed. L. Balter (Santa Barbara, CA: ABC-CLIO, 2001), 320–22.

5. "Human Behavior as Animal Behavior," in *The Behavior of Animals: Mechanisms, Function and Evolution*, eds. J. J. Bolhuis and L. A Giraldeau (Oxford, England: Blackwell, 2005), 393–408.

6. Stan Finger, "Police Take Emaciated Girls from House," *Wichita Eagle*, July 22, 2006.

On the Web

CHILDREN AND DIVORCE

kidshealth.org/parent/emotions/feelings/help_child_divorce.html. Provides practical information on three sites for parents, kids, and teens. Site is supported by the Nemours Foundation.

www.billsarena.com. A Web site designed by a youngster for other children who are experiencing the divorce of their parents.

www.childrenofdivorce.com. This is the Web site of a therapist in Los Angeles. It lists distress signs that may be observed in children.

www.divorceinfo.com/children.htm. The "Getting Your Children through Your Divorce" page of the Divorceinfo.com Web site contains information (and links to other pages) for helping children; there's a special page for adult children of divorce called "When the 'Kids' Aren't Kids."

www.divorcereform.org/all.html. This site, sponsored by the Americans for Divorce Reform, contains links to abstracts of studies on children of divorce.

www.gocrc.com. Web site of the Children's Rights Council, a national nonprofit organization protecting children's rights. Deals with emotions and personal stories.

www.helpguide.org/mental/children_divorce.htm. This page—Coping with Divorce: Helping Your Child Cope with Separation or Divorce—describes the short-term effects of divorce on children and offers help for children during and following divorce.

www.kidsturn.org. Web site for children to talk about and share divorce experiences. Includes a Kids' Divorce Help Page.

www.kidsturncentral.com/topics/issues/divorce.htm. The "Children of Divorce" page on Kids' Turn Central contains many resources for children that "are meant to assist both kids going through divorce—and kids who want to help understand what a friend might be going through."

www.sandcastlesprogram.com. A group experience designed to assist children in dealing with their parents' divorce.

www.talk-about it.com. Specially designed cards to help a child discuss the troubling issues and feelings they have about divorce.

DIVORCE AND WOMEN

www.divorce-and-money.com/divorced-women.shtml. A financial analysis looks at the years following divorce, helping people see what can be expected.

www.divorceandwomen.com. Woman's Divorce: Helping Women Survive Divorce and Rebuild Their Lives is an online resource center for women. This Web site is written by a former family law lawyer, and the goal is to help "women take control of their divorce."

www.enotalone.com. The Not Alone Web site features articles on what women can expect after divorce.

www.selfgrowth.com/articles/Augustine11.html. Article on how women should protect themselves financially regarding divorce.

www.womansdivorce.com. Site provides information about legal and children's issues and financial survival for women.

DIVORCE AND MEN

www.acfc.org. The American Coalition for Fathers and Children has an extensive site with considerable information on a number of topics. The coalition directs its efforts to the creation of a family law system, legislative system, and public awareness that promotes equal rights for all parties affected by divorce and the breakup of a family or establishment of paternity.

www.divorcedfather.com. This site offers information for fathers experiencing a divorce.

www.fatherhood.org. The purpose of the National Fatherhood Initiative is to improve the well-being of children by increasing the proportion of children growing up with involved, responsible, and committed fathers.

www.fathersrights.org. Pro bono hints to help fathers win divorce, child custody, and support battles and defeat false allegations of domestic violence or child abuse.

www.ncfcnh.org. This is the Web site of the National Congress for Fathers and Children. The mission of this organization is to preserve relationships between fathers and their children.

www.thisisby.us/index.php/custody_ingay_divorce. A description of the divorce process for gay married men with a discussion of custody by gay fathers.

SINGLE PARENTS

www.parentswithoutpartners.org. Parents without Partners is an international, nonprofit, educational organization devoted to the interests of single parents and their children.

www.singlemothers.org. Web site of the National Organization of Single Mothers, Inc., which is devoted to helping mothers who are single by choice or chance.

www.singleparentusa.com. The Single Parent Resource Center is a clearinghouse for information on single parent organizations in the United States and around the world.

The goal is to enable single parent groups and organizations to share information on program development, service models, and techniques and to facilitate referral of single parents to groups or support programs in their local communities.

STEPFAMILIES

www.childparenting.about.com/od/stepparenting. About.com's stepparenting forum offers information on many topics for parents and stepparents.

www.saafamilies.org. Web site sponsored by Stepfamily Association of America, Inc.

www.stepfamily.net. The Stepfamily Network is a forum for stepfamilies that offers support and information.

www.stepfamily.org. The Stepfamily Foundation is devoted to the issues that are involved with the dynamics of stepfamilies and blended families.

PARENTING THROUGH DIVORCE

hometown.aol.com/famtogetherusa. Organization dedicated to helping families stay together after divorce.

www.divorcenet.com. This page on Divorcenet.com offers advice on postdivorce parenting.

www.divorcesource.com. Describes how children are affected by divorce and what parents can do to help.

www.divorcesupport.com. Web site helps with parenting through divorce.

www.eap.partners.org/WorkLife/Life_Transitions/Life_Transitions_Intro/Life_Transitions_Intro.asp. Parenting through divorce.

www.onetoughjob.org. Practical advice on parenting.

www.spig.clara.net. The mission of the Shared Parenting Information Group is to promote responsible shared parenting after separation and divorce. This Web site offers information, research, and resources.

PARENTAL ALIENATION

www.deltabravo.net. Parental Alienation Information Archive. All the information on the Separated Parenting Access & Resource Center site regarding parental alienation has been consolidated on this central reference page. New articles are at the top of the page. You can use the drop-down box to select an article or browse from a list.

www.education.mcgill.ca/pain. The Parental Alienation Information Network provides links to articles and providers of services.

www.feminista.com/archives/v1n2/wilson.html. Explains parental alienation syndrome and why it is so often used against mothers.

www.leadershipcouncil.org/1/pas/1.html. This page of the Leadership Council on Child Abuse & Interpersonal Violence Web site contains articles and information on parental alienation syndrome as utilized in child custody battles.

www.parentalalienation.org. Information on parental alienation syndrome and useful links to similar sites.

www.rgardner.com. Richard A. Gardner's site—the innovator of the term parental alienation syndrome.

CUSTODY

family.findlaw.com/divorce/divorce-children/children-reaction.html. This site offers information on a variety of divorce-related topics including child custody.

womansdivorce.com/children-and-divorce.html. The Web site discusses some of the issues that women face concerning children and divorce, such as custody, visitation, child support, and resolving conflicts.

www.childcustody.org. Childcustody.org is a member of the Child Custody Network and is dedicated to the best interests of children. Contains links to over 100 child custody sites.

www.childcustodylibrary.com. The Child Custody Library is a resource for help and information on topics pertaining to child custody.

www.childrenofdivorce.com. Helpful child custody information and advice relating to custody, visitation, child support, and other issues related to children and divorce.

www.cooking-italian-food.com/newbook.htm. The Custodial/Non-Custodial Parent Record Keeper is designed to help keep documentation in order to help the court determine "what's in the best interest of the children."

www.custody911.com. Provides links to over 100 child custody Web sites, which cover subjects such as custody evaluations, child support, and custody for fathers and custody for mothers.

www.custodyreform.com. Custody Reform is committed to fairness in the child custody process. The Web site contains resources for noncustodial parents.

www.custodysource.com. This site lists individuals, groups, and organizations to help with the difficult challenges of child custody. For fathers, mothers, and grandparents.

www.parentingplan.net. Parenting Plan is a site where all the available information on creating a parent plan has been consolidated.

www.svdirectory.com. Directory of supervised visitation facilities.

MEDIATION

www.divorceandfinance.com. The Association of Divorce Financial Planners' site contains information on finding a financial planner.

www.mediate.com/articles/boskey.cfm. Links to Web sites that are good starting points when seeking information on alternative dispute resolution.

www.nfm.org.uk. The National Family Mediation Service of Britain provides information about local mediation services to help couples resolve practical difficulties with minimum conflict.

www.okparent.org/fam_trans/Maritalproblems.htm. An index to family mediation–related Web sites.

GUIDE TO FAMILY LAW

family.findlaw.com/divorce/divorce-children/children-reaction.html. FindLaw's legal information, tools, and resources are free. Entering one's ZIP code narrows the information to articles, links, and attorney listings that are relevant for one's area.

GENERAL INFORMATION

groups.msn.com/divorcecaresupport. A community Web site for people going through divorce. Message board, chat room, poetry, book club, and general resources.

meghann10.tripod.com/agunw. Support group Web site for adults who grew up in divorced households and are now trying to build families of their own.

womansdivorce.com. The Web site discusses some of the issues that people face concerning children and divorce, such as custody, visitation, child support, and resolving conflicts.

www.been-dumped.com. The Been-Dumped Web site shares the hurt from a broken relationship. For those who are separated from a partner, divorced, or just lonely and want to talk and share advice with people in similar situations.

www.betterdivorce.com. Presents resources to help moderate divorce. Information on statistics, custody, effects of divorce on children, conflict resolution, divorce rituals, and emotional support.

www.divorceasfriends.com. Divorce as Friends is a Web site that contains articles, resources, and support to help minimize conflict "and possibly save your marriage."

www.divorcedirectory.com/index.shtml. A resource that offers services and guidance, from lawyers to self-help books to dating services.

www.divorceinfo.com. Offers advice on survival skills during a divorce and suggestions for saving money, time, and pain in divorce; coping with pain; managing lawyers in divorce; keeping control; and dealing with property division, child support, alimony, and taxes.

www.divorceinteractive.com. A free and confidential Web site devoted to disseminating divorce materials that will help parents going through a divorce to cooperate and "build a better future for themselves and their children." DivorceInteractive.com provides survival tools, information, and resources. There is a section in which you can access information particular to each state.

www.divorcemagazine.com. Self-help resource for those seeking information about separation and divorce.

www.divorcenet.com. DivorceNet.com is a Web site dedicated to helping people through the painful process of divorce and divorce-related issues. It offers a nationwide directory of divorce lawyers, mediators, and financial professionals; an online community; and a divorce library.

www.divorcenter.org/resources. A directory of divorce-related Web sites and resources, including support groups, a guide to professionals, suggested readings, and more.

www.divorce-online.co.uk. Web site about divorce and related issues contains links to Web sites in the United Kingdom, United States, and European Union. Considered the leading self-help divorce Web site for the United States and Canada.

www.divorcereform.org. Information on divorce and reconciliation.

www.divorcesource.com. Divorce Source contains a variety of divorce-related resources and Web sites.

www.divorcesupport.com. DivorceSupport.com is a support site for people experiencing, divorce, dissolution, separation, and issues of custody, alimony, and visitation. Contains lists of divorce professionals to help you in your area.

www.divorcetransitions.com. Site presents basic information on separation, divorce, divorce recovery, and starting over single.

www.enotalone.com. Web site that has articles and a discussion board devoted to divorce.

www.guidetodivorce.com. Web site designed to answer questions about divorce

www.ssa.gov/gethelp1.htm and www.nob.com/article.cfm. A nonprofit membership organization of divorced and separated individuals in the Washington, D.C., area. Includes events, FAQ, links, and contact details.

www.womansdivorce.com/moving-on-after-divorce.html. This site is geared toward helping women cope with a divorce, with essays and information.

Bibliography

Amato, P. R. "Children's Adjustment to Divorce: Theories, Hypotheses, and Empirical Support." *Journal of Marriage and the Family* 55, no. 1 (1993): 23–38.

Amato, P. R. "The Consequence of Divorce for Adults and Children." *Journal of Marriage and Family* 62, no. 4 (2000): 1269.

Amato, P. R., and S. J. Rogers. "A Longitudinal Study of Marital Problems and Subsequent Divorce." *Journal of Marriage and the Family* 59, no. 3 (1997): 612–24.

American Psychiatric Association. *Diagnostic and Statistical Manual of Mental Disorders*, 4th ed. Washington, DC: American Psychiatric Association, 2000.

Anonymous. *Twelve Steps: Twelve Traditions*. New York: Alcoholics Anonymous World Services, 1996.

Arnold, Sir Edwin. "The Light of Asia." In *A Victorian Anthology, 1837–1895*, ed. E. C. Stedman. Cambridge, England: Riverside Press, 1895.

Bacon, F. *Essays, Civil and Moral*. Harvard Classics, Vol. 3, Part 1. New York: P. F. Collier, 1909–14.

Bettelheim, B. *A Good Enough Parent*. New York: Alfred A. Knopf, 1987.

Booth, A., and P. Amato. "Divorce and Psychological Stress." *American Sociological Association Journal of Health and Social Behavior* 32, no. 4 (1991): 396–407.

Bradshaw, J. *The Family*. Deerfield Beach, FL: Health Communications, 1988.

Bramlett, M. D., and W. D. Mosher. "First Marriage Dissolution, Divorce and Remarriage: United States." National Center for Health Statistics, Department of Health and Human Services, Centers for Disease Control and Prevention, National Center for Health Statistics. Hyattsville, MD: Department of Health and Human Services, Center for Disease Control and Prevention, National Center for Health Statistics, 2001.

Brooke, J. "Home Alone Together." *New York Times*, May 4, 2006, D5.

Buchanan, C., and others. "Caught between Parents: Adolescents' Experience in Divorced Homes." *Journal of Early Adolescence* 62, no. 5 (1991): 1008–29.

Buchanan, C., M. Buchanan, and others. *Adolescence after Divorce*. Cambridge, MA: Harvard University Press, 1996.

Buehler, C., and J. M. Gerard. "Divorce Law in the United States: A Focus on Child Custody." *Family Relations* 44, no. 4 (1995): 439–58.

Buehlman, K. T., J. Gottman, and F. Katz. "How a Couple Views Their Past Predicts Their Future: Predicting Divorce from an Oral History." *Journal of Family Psychology* 5, no. 3–4 (1992): 295–318.

Burns, A., and C. Scot. *Mother Headed Families and Why They Have Increased*. Hillsdale, NJ: Lawrence Erlbaum, 1994.

Camara, K., and G. Resnick. "Interparental Conflict and Cooperation: Factors Moderating Children's Post-Divorce Adjustment." In *Impact of Divorce, Single Parenting, and Step-parenting on Children*, ed. E. Mavis Hetherington and Josephine D. Arasteh. Hillsdale, NJ: Lawrence Erlbaum Associates, 1989.

"Children's Living Arrangements," *U.S. Census Reports on Living Arrangements of Children* 2, no. 4 (July/August 2001). Available at http://www.census.gov/2003pubs/p20-547.pdf.

Cookston, J. T. "Parental Supervision and Family Structure: Effects on Adolescent Problem Behaviors." *Journal of Divorce and Remarriage* 32, no. 1/2 (1999): 107–22.

Coysh, W. S., J. R. Johnston, J. M. Tschann, J. S. Wallerstein, and M. Kline. "Parental Post Divorce Adjustment in Joint and Sole Physical Custody Families. *Journal of Family Issues* 10, no. 1 (1989): 52–71.

Craig, W. J., ed. *Hamlet* 2.2.232. *The Complete Works of William Shakespeare*. London: Oxford University Press, 1914.

Daly, M., and M. Wilson. "Infanticide." In *Parenthood in America: An Encyclopedia*, ed. L. Balter. Santa Barbara, CA: ABC-CLIO, 2001, 320–322.

Demo, D. H., and A. C. Acock. "The Impact of Divorce on Children." *Journal of Marriage and the Family* 50, no. 3 (1988): 619–48.

Dickinson, E. *The Complete Poems of Emily Dickinson*. Boston: Little, Brown, 1924.

Divorce Lawyer Source, http://www.divorce-lawyer-source.com.

Donner, M. B. "Tearing the Child Apart: The Contribution of Narcissism, Envy, and Perverse Modes of Thought to Child Custody Wars." *Psychoanalytic Psychology* 23, no. 3 (2006): 542–53.

Ehrenberg, M. F. "Couples Who Make It Work." *Journal of Divorce and Remarriage* 26, no. 1/2 (1996): 93–113.

Elkind, D. *Grandparenting: Understanding Today's Children*. Glenview, IL: Scott, Foresman, 1990.

Emery, R. *Marriage, Divorce, and Children's Adjustment*. Newbury Park, CA: Sage, 1988.

Emery, R. *Marriage, Divorce, and Children's Adjustment*. 2nd ed. Thousand Oaks, CA: Sage, 1999.

Fay, J., and F. Cline. *Grandparenting with Love and Logic*. Golden, CO: Love and Logic Press, 1994.

Finley, G. E., and S. J. Schwartz. "Bales Revisited: Young Adult Children's Characterization of the Fathering Role." *APA Journal-Psychology of Men & Masculinity* 7, no. 1 (2006): 42–55.

Fisher, H. E. *Anatomy of Love: The Natural History of Monogamy, Adultery and Divorce*. New York: Simon & Schuster, 1992.

Friends in Recovery. *The 12 Steps for Adult Children*. San Diego, CA: Recovery Publications, 1987.

Gamerman, E. "Mism@tched.com." *Wall Street Journal*, April 1–2, 2006, 1, 4.

Gardner, R. *The Parental Alienation Syndrome: A Guide for Mental Health and Legal Professionals*. Cresskill, NJ: Creative Therapeutic, 1992.

Glen, N. D., and K. B. Kramer. "The Marriage and Divorce of the Children of Divorce." *Journal of Marriage and Family* 44 (1987): 335–47.

Goode, W., and J. World. *World Changes in Divorce Patterns*. New Haven, CT: Yale University Press, 1993.

Gruber, J. "Is Making Divorce Easier Bad for Children? The Long-Run Implications of Unilateral Divorce." *Journal of Labor Economics* 22 (2004): 799–833.

Guidubaldi, J., J. D. Perry, and B. Nastasi. "Children's Adjustment." In *Applied Social Psychology Annual*, ed. S. Oskamp. Vol. 7: *Family Processes and Problems*. Newbury Park, CA: Sage Publications, 1987.

Hayslip, B., and J. Patrick. *Working with Custodial Grandparents*. New York: Springer Publishing, 2003.

Hayslip, B., Jr., and R. Goldberg, eds. *Grandparents Raising Grandchildren*. New York: Springer Publishing, 2000.

Herrmann, A. "Child-Rearing: Research Explores Changes in Household Dynamic." *Chicago Sun-Times* Metro Section, May 3, 2007, 26–27.

Hetherington, E. M., and J. D. Arasteh, eds. *Custody of Children Following Divorce: Impact of Divorce, Single Parenting and Step-parenting on Children*. Hillsdale, NJ: Lawrence Erlbaum, 1988.

Hetherington, E. M., M. Stanley-Hagan, and E. R. Anderson. "Marital Transitions: A Child's Perspective." *American Psychologist* 44, no. 2 (1989): 303–12.

James, J., and R. Friedman. *When Children Grieve: For Adults to Help Children Deal with Death, Divorce, Pet Loss, Moving and Other Losses*. New York: HarperCollins, 2002.

Kaufman, L. "In Custody Fights, A Hurdle for the Poor." *New York Times*, April 8, 2007, 21.

Kelly, J., and E. M. Hetherington. *For Better or for Worse*. New York: W. W. Norton, 2002.

Knowlton, L. "The Resilience of Children in the Face of Trauma." *Psychiatric Times* 18, no. 4 (2001): 1.

Kornhaber, A. *The Grandparent's Guide*. New York: Contemporary Books, 2002.

Kornhaber, A. *The Grandparent Solution*. San Francisco, CA: Jossey-Bass, 2004.

Lamb, M. E., K. J. Sternberg, and R. A. Thompson. "The Effects of Divorce and Custody Arrangements on Children's Behavior, Development, and Adjustment." *Family Court Review* 35, no. 4 (1997): 393–404.

Maccoby, E. E., C. Buchanan, R. H. Buchanan, and S. M. Dornbusch. "Postdivorce Roles of Mothers and Fathers in the Lives of Children." *Journal of Family Psychology* 7 (1993): 24–38.

Maccoby, E. E., C. E. Depner, and R. H. Mnookin. "Coparenting in the Second Year after Divorce." *Journal of Marriage and the Family* 52 (1991): 141–55.

Maccoby, E. E., and R. H. Mnookin. *Dividing the Child: Social and Legal Dilemmas of Custody*. Cambridge, MA: Harvard University Press, 1992.

Mavers, L. "The La's." *I Can't Sleep*. Universal Music Group. Cassette recording B00005953B. London, 1990.

McGregor, J. "Love & Money." *Smart Money Magazine*, February 9, 2004, http://www.smartmoney.com.

Morgan, L. W. "Child Support Guidelines and the Shared Custody Dilemma." *Divorce Litigation*, November 1998, http://www.childsupportguidelines.com/articles/art199906.html.

Nakonezny, P. A., R. D. Schull, and J. L. Rodgers. "The Effect of No-Fault Divorce Law on the Divorce Rate across the 50 States and Its Relation to Income, Education and Religiosity." *Journal of Marriage and the Family* 57, no. 2 (1995): 477–88.

National Institutes of Health. *Brief Notes on the Mental Health of Children and Adolescents*. Bethesda, MD: NIH, 1999, http://www.medhelp.org/NIHlib/GF-233.html.

National Institutes of Health. *Fact Sheet: Going to Extremes, Bipolar Disorder*. Bethesda, MD: NIH, 2001.

National Institutes of Health. *Progressive Brain Changes Detected in Childhood Onset Schizophrenia*. Press Release. Bethesda, MD: NIH, 1997.

Navarro, M. "A Family Feud That Is Familiar." *New York Times*, March 11, 2007, 1, 10.

Parent Place. *Going to Grandma's House . . . to Live*. Springfield, IL: Parent Place, 2001.

Perrine, S. "Keeping Divorced Dad's at a Distance." *New York Times*, June 18, 2006, 13.

Peterson, R. R. "A Re-Evaluation of the Economic Consequences of Divorce." *American Sociological Review* 61, no. 3 (1996): 528–36.

Pew Research Center. *As Marriage and Parenthood Drift Apart, Public Is Concerned about Social Impact: Generation Gap in Values, Behaviors*. Available at http://www.pewresearch.org/pubs/526/Marriage-parenthood.

Pruett, M. K., and K. Hoganbruen. "Joint Custody and Shared Parenting." *Child and Adolescent Psychiatric Clinics of North America* 7, no. 2 (1998): 273–93.

Pruett, M. K., and C. Santangel. "Joint Custody and Empirical Knowledge: The Estranged Bedfellows of Divorce." In *The Scientific Basis of Custody Decisions*, ed. R. M. Galatzer-Levy. New York: Wiley, 1999.

Reissman, C. K. *Divorce Talk: Women and Men Make Sense of Personal Relationships*. Piscataway, NJ: Rutgers University Press, 1990.

Rodgers, B. "Pathways between Parental Divorce and Adult Depression." *Journal of Child Psychology and Psychiatry* 35, no. 7 (1994): 289–308.

Saluter, A. *Marital Status and Living Arrangements*. Washington, DC: U.S. Census Bureau, Series P20–484, 1994. Available at http://www.census.gov/population/www/pop-profile/msla.htm/.

Seltzer, J. A., and Y. Brandreth. "What Fathers Say about Involvement with Children after Separation." *Journal of Family Issues* 15, no. 1 (1994): 49–77.

Seltzer, J. A., N. C. Schaeffer, and H. Charng. "Family Ties after Divorce: The Relationship between Visiting and Paying Child Support." *Journal of Marriage and the Family* 51 (1989): 1013–32.

SixWise.com. *The Top 5 Things Couples Argue About*, 2007, http://www.sixwise.com/newsletters/06/02/22/the_top_5_things_couples_argue_about.htm.

Stewart, S. D. "Disneyland Dads, Disneyland Moms: How Nonresident Parents Spend Time with Absent Children." *Journal of Family Issues* 20, no. 4 (1999): 539–56.

"Story Corps." *Morning Edition*, National Public Radio, January 27, 2006, http://www.npr.org/templates/story/story.php?storyId=5173527.

Strom, R., and S. Strom. *Becoming a Better Grandparent*. Thousand Oaks, CA: Sage Publications, 1991.

Sweeper, S., and K. Halford. "Assessing Adult Adjustment to Relationship Separation: The Psychological Adjustment to Separation Test (PAST)." *Journal of Family Psychology* 20, no. 4 (2006): 632–40.

Turner, J. *Encyclopedia of Relationships across the Lifespan*. Westport, CT: Greenwood Press, 1996.

U.S. Department of Health and Human Services. *Mental Health: A Report of the Surgeon General*. Rockville, MD: U.S. DHHS, 1999.

Wallerstein, J. S. "The Long-Term Effects of Divorce on Children: A Review." *Journal of the American Academy of Child Adolescent Psychiatry* 3, no. 6 (1991): 1022–3.

Wallerstein, J. S., J. B. Kelly, and S. Blakeslee. *Surviving the Breakup: How Children and Parents Cope with Divorce*. New York: Basic Books, 1996.

Weiss, Y., and R. J. Willis. "Children as Collective Goods and Divorce Settlements." *Journal of Labor Economics* 3 (1985): 268–92.

Wilson, E. O. *Sociobiology: The New Synthesis* (25th anniversary ed.). New Haven, CT: Yale University Press, 1975.

Woititz, J. G. *Adult Children of Alcoholics*. Hollywood, FL: Health Communications, 1983.

Zaslow, M. J. "Sex Differences in Children's Response to Parental Divorce: Samples, Variables, Ages, and Sources." *American Journal of Orthopsychiatry* 59, no. 1 (1989): 118–41.

Zill, N., R. D. Morrison, and M. J. Coiro. "Long-Term Effects of Parental Divorce on Parent-Child Relationships, Adjustment, and Achievement in Young Adulthood: Families in Transition." *Journal of Family Psychology* 7, no. 1 (1993): 91–103.

Zinner, R. "Joint Physical Custody: Smart Solution or Problematic Plan?" Divorce Headquarters, 1998, http://www.divorcehq.com/articles/jointcustody.html.

Index

About the Authors

JESSICA G. LIPPMAN is a private practice clinical psychologist with nearly 30 years of experience, much of that with mothers, fathers, and children facing or in the midst of divorce. She is an adjunct assistant professor at Northwestern Medical School. Lippman and co-author Paddy Lewis regularly appear in media and have been interviewed by publications including *The Wall Street Journal*, *London Times*, and *Chicago Tribune*.

PADDY GREENWALL LEWIS is a recently retired clinical psychologist, whose private practice often included couples and families facing divorce issues. She also served 10 years as the chief psychologist at the Michael Reese Hospital & Medical Center in Chicago. With Lippman, she co-authored an earlier book, *Helping Children Cope with the Death of a Parent: A Guide for the First Year* (Praeger, 2004).